Ultimate POUND CAKES

—≫ CLASSIC RECIPE COLLECTION ≪—

83 PRESS

Ultimate POUND CAKES

CLASSIC RECIPE COLLECTION

Hoffman Media
1900 International Park Drive, Suite 50
Birmingham, Alabama 35243
hoffmanmedia.com

ISBN # 978-1-940772-47-9
Printed in China

ON THE COVER:
Tres Leches Pound Cake, page 44.

83
PRESS

contents

introduction

Pound cake is proof that something old can be made new again. From heirloom recipes to current variations, the *Ultimate Pound Cakes: Classic Recipe Collection* will give you a treasure trove of over 100 recipes to choose from. Holidays, special occasions, or weeknight suppers, these test-kitchen approved, home-baked cakes are always a welcome surprise for

family and friends. They also make fabulous gifts. The pound cake has grown from its early

18th century English origin to a variety show of flavors with sour cream, chocolates, caramel,

and spice to name a few. From tube cakes to mini loaves, this beautiful selection of recipes will

enhance your table with delicious desserts for years to come!

Phyllis Hoffman DePiano

Rooted in humble beginnings, the pound cake has risen from its original four-ingredient version to complex flavorful masterpieces worthy of any celebration. We aren't completely sure who made the very first pound cake, but we sure are thankful for them. This simple yet elegant cake gets its name from the amount of each ingredient—a pound of flour, eggs, butter, and sugar, which would yield a cake large enough to feed several families. This is what was counted on back in the 18th century, when the recipe first appeared in print. Baking ingredients were hard to come by, so sharing goods was certainly appealing. Nowadays, we have the luxury of baking half-pound cakes in any flavor we prefer. But, our desire for this dense, richly flavored cake has not diminished over the years.

Although this recipe has English origins, it has become an unequivocal American classic. Author Amelia Simmons penned the first pound cake recipe in America in her book, *American Cookery*. Her rendition included rosewater—a flavor that must've been popular during its publication in 1796. However, methods and ingredients (like baking powder and lard) have changed over time to suit evolving tastes. Along with new ingredients, proportions of the basic ingredients were adjusted to make a smaller, less dense cake. While this basic cake no longer has a pound per ingredient, the name stuck. Through the decades, traditional pound cake has become recognized as a basic cake along with fruitcake, spice cake, sponge cake, and angel food cake. These delightful desserts all form a strong foundation for so many of our modern confections.

That strong foundation was enhanced tremendously in the mid-19th century when baking powder was introduced, revolutionizing the baking world. People no longer had to rely on eggs alone as their leavening (rising) agent. Once home bakers got their hands on baking powder, there wasn't a need for so many eggs. Another new kitchen ingredient was shortening—a mixture of lard and butter. The combination of baking powder and shortening definitely diminished the need for one pound each of eggs and butter. The introduction of these convenience products brought around a new class of cakes called composition cakes. These cakes were great for bakers on a budget and didn't take nearly as much time to prepare. With the addition of these revolutionary ingredients, the world of cake baking was introduced to middle class America for the very first time. Through the years, the availability of certain additives like almond and vanilla extracts, dried pineapple, chopped nuts, or even lemon-lime soda allowed for pound cakes to expand their flavor profiles and texture.

In this book, you will explore pound cake in its many forms, flavors, and fashions. These pages are filled with over 100 recipes and show a bevy of cake pan options to be enjoyed—tube, Bundt, cast iron, loaf, and more! You will see basic pound cakes with classic, buttery flavors and compact crumbs, and a wide variety of flavorful additives and decorative flourishes that make each cake a homemade masterpiece. Pound cakes have become the highlight of holidays and entertaining, and they also make fabulous gifts. Home-baked treats are always a welcome surprise for friends and loved ones. These cakes are a perennial favorite with home bakers and will look stunning on the sideboard at your next fête.

Grandma's Favorite
Pound Cake, page 18.

tube cakes

Pound cakes are traditionally baked in
straight-sided tube pans. The tube pan is loved
for the golden crust it gives to these
traditional, moist cakes.

Original Pound Cake

1½ cups unsalted butter, softened
2½ cups sugar
1   tablespoon cornstarch
3   cups all-purpose flour, sifted and divided
8   large eggs, divided
½   teaspoon vanilla extract
Garnish: whipped cream, sliced fresh strawberries

Preheat oven to 325°. Spray a 10-inch tube pan with baking spray with flour.

In a large bowl, beat butter, sugar, and cornstarch with a mixer at medium speed until fluffy, 3 to 4 minutes, stopping to scrape sides of bowl. Add 1 cup flour, and beat for 1 minute. Add 4 eggs, and beat for 1 minute. Add remaining 2 cups flour, and beat just until combined. Add remaining 4 eggs, and beat until combined. Stir in vanilla. Spoon batter into prepared pan.

Bake for 1 hour. Increase oven temperature to 350°, and bake 15 minutes more. Let cool in pan for 10 minutes. Remove from pan, and let cool completely on a wire rack. Garnish with whipped cream and strawberries, if desired.

cake tip
Don't open the oven door until your cake has baked for at least three-fourths of the recommended baking time. The rush of cold air that hits the cake when the door is opened could cause the cake to collapse.

Grandma's Favorite Pound Cake

1   cup unsalted butter, softened
½   cup butter-flavored shortening
3   cups sugar
5   large eggs
3   cups all-purpose flour
½   teaspoon salt
½   teaspoon baking powder
1   cup whole buttermilk
1   teaspoon vanilla extract
½   teaspoon almond extract
½   teaspoon coconut extract

Preheat oven to 325°. Spray a 10-inch tube pan with baking spray with flour.

In a large bowl, beat butter, shortening, and sugar with a mixer at medium speed until fluffy, 3 to 4 minutes, stopping to scrape sides of bowl. Add eggs, one at a time, beating well after each addition.

In a medium bowl, sift together flour, salt, and baking powder. In a small bowl, combine buttermilk and extracts.

Reduce mixer speed to low. Gradually add flour mixture to butter mixture alternately with buttermilk mixture, beginning and ending with flour mixture, beating just until combined after each addition. Pour batter into prepared pan. Tap pan on counter to release any air bubbles.

Bake for 45 minutes. Cover with foil, and bake until a wooden pick inserted near center comes out clean, about 45 minutes more. Let cool in pan for 20 minutes. Remove from pan, and let cool completely on a wire rack. Store in an airtight container at room temperature for up to 3 days.

cake tip
All the ingredients (except buttermilk) should be at room temperature before you begin mixing. Butter and eggs at room temperature will blend together more easily and will ensure that you get good results.

Honey Almond Pound Cake

Cake

1 (8-ounce) package cream cheese, softened
1½ cups unsalted butter, softened
2½ cups sugar
3 cups all-purpose flour, divided
6 large eggs, divided
1 teaspoon almond extract
Honey Citrus Syrup (recipe follows)
⅓ cup honey
½ cup toasted sliced almonds

Honey Citrus Syrup
Makes about ⅔ cup

1 cup water
½ cup sugar
½ orange, cut into ¼-inch-thick slices
½ lemon, cut into ¼-inch-thick slices
1 cinnamon stick
¼ cup honey

Preheat oven to 325°. Spray a 12-cup tube pan with baking spray with flour.

Cake: In a large bowl, beat cream cheese and butter with a mixer at medium speed until creamy. Add sugar; beat until fluffy, 3 to 4 minutes, stopping to scrape sides of bowl. Reduce mixer speed to low. Add 1 cup flour, beating until combined. Add 2 eggs, beating just until yellow disappears. Repeat procedure twice with remaining 2 cups flour and remaining 4 eggs. Beat in almond extract. Pour batter into prepared pan.

Bake until a wooden pick inserted near center comes out clean, 1 hour and 20 minutes to 1½ hours. Using an 8-inch wooden skewer, pierce holes ½ inch apart in warm cake. Slowly pour warm Honey Citrus Syrup over cake, allowing cake to absorb syrup. Let cool in pan for 15 minutes. Remove from pan, and drizzle with honey. Sprinkle with almonds. Let cool completely on a wire rack.

Honey Citrus Syrup: In medium saucepan, bring 1 cup water, sugar, orange slices, lemon slices, and cinnamon stick to boil over medium heat. Reduce heat, and simmer for 30 minutes. Strain mixture into small bowl. Stir in honey, and keep warm.

Ultimate Cream Cheese-Vanilla Bean Pound Cake

MAKES ABOUT 16 SERVINGS

1 (8-ounce) package cream cheese, softened
1 cup unsalted butter, softened
3 cups granulated sugar
6 large eggs
1 vanilla bean, split lengthwise, seeds scraped and reserved
1 tablespoon vanilla extract
3½ cups all-purpose flour
1 teaspoon baking powder
½ teaspoon salt
1 cup heavy whipping cream
Garnish: confectioners' sugar

Preheat oven to 325°. Spray a 10-inch tube pan with baking spray with flour.

In the bowl of a stand mixer fitted with the paddle attachment, beat cream cheese and butter at medium speed until creamy. Add granulated sugar; beat until fluffy, 3 to 4 minutes, stopping to scrape sides of bowl. Add eggs, one at a time, beating well after each addition. Beat in vanilla bean seeds and vanilla extract.

In a large bowl, whisk together flour, baking powder, and salt. Reduce mixer speed to low. Gradually add flour mixture to butter mixture alternately with cream, beginning and ending with flour mixture, beating just until combined after each addition. Spoon batter into prepared pan.

Bake until a wooden pick inserted near center comes out clean, 1 hour and 20 minutes to 1½ hours, covering with foil halfway through baking to prevent excess browning, if necessary. Let cool in pan for 10 minutes. Remove from pan, and let cool completely on a wire rack. Garnish with confectioners' sugar, if desired.

Carrot Pound Cake

Cake

1	(8-ounce) package cream cheese, softened
1½	cups unsalted butter, softened
3	cups sugar
3	cups all-purpose flour
1	teaspoon ground cinnamon
6	large eggs, divided
1	teaspoon vanilla extract
½	teaspoon lemon extract
2	cups shredded carrot
1	cup chopped pecans

Lemon Glaze (recipe follows)

Lemon Glaze
Makes about ¾ cup

⅔	cup confectioners' sugar
1	tablespoon whole milk
¼	teaspoon lemon extract

Preheat oven to 325°. Spray a 12-cup tube pan with baking spray with flour.

Cake: In large bowl, beat cream cheese and butter with a mixer at medium speed until creamy. Add sugar; beat until fluffy, 3 to 4 minutes, stopping to scrape sides of bowl.

In a medium bowl, whisk together flour and cinnamon. Reduce mixer speed to low. Add 1 cup flour mixture to butter mixture, beating until combined. Add 2 eggs, beating just until yellow disappears. Repeat procedure twice with remaining 2 cups flour mixture and remaining 4 eggs. Stir in extracts. Fold in carrot and pecans. Pour batter into prepared pan.

Bake until wooden pick inserted near center comes out clean, about 1½ hours. Let cool in pan for 10 minutes. Remove from pan, and let cool completely on a wire rack. Drizzle cooled cake with Lemon Glaze.

Lemon Glaze: In small bowl, stir together confectioners' sugar, milk, and lemon extract until smooth.

Buttery Champagne Pound Cake

Cake
1½ cups unsalted butter,
    softened
2½ cups sugar
5   large eggs
3½ cups all-purpose flour
½   teaspoon baking powder
¼   teaspoon salt
1¼ cups Champagne,
    or sparkling wine
Champagne Glaze
    (recipe follows)
Garnish: fresh raspberries

Champagne Glaze
Makes about 1 cup
1   cup sugar
½   cup unsalted butter
½   cup Champagne,
    or sparkling wine
¼   cup water

Spray a 10-inch tube pan with baking spray with flour.

Cake: In the bowl of a stand mixer fitted with the paddle attachment, beat butter and sugar at medium speed until fluffy, 3 to 4 minutes, stopping to scrape sides of bowl. Add eggs, one at a time, beating well after each addition. Reduce mixer speed to low.

In a medium bowl, whisk together flour, baking powder, and salt. Gradually add flour mixture to butter mixture alternately with Champagne, beginning and ending with flour mixture, beating just until combined after each addition. Spoon batter into prepared pan.

Place pan in a cold oven. Bake at 325° until a wooden pick inserted near center comes out clean, 1 hour and 10 minutes to 1 hour and 20 minutes, covering with foil halfway through baking to prevent excess browning, if necessary. Let cool in pan for 10 minutes. Using a wooden skewer, poke holes all over top of cake. Gradually pour half of Champagne Glaze over cake. Let stand for 30 minutes. Remove from pan, and gradually pour remaining glaze over cake. Let cool completely on a wire rack. Garnish with raspberries, if desired.

Champagne Glaze: In a medium saucepan, combine all ingredients. Bring to a boil over medium-high heat; reduce heat, and simmer for 5 minutes, stirring occasionally. Remove from heat, and let cool to room temperature.

Rum Raisin Pound Cake

Cake
½   cup spiced rum
½   cup raisins
½   cup golden raisins
2   cups unsalted butter,
      softened
1   cup granulated sugar
1   cup firmly packed brown
      sugar
6   large eggs
1   (14-ounce) can sweetened
      condensed milk
½   cup whole milk
1   tablespoon vanilla extract
4   cups all-purpose flour
1½ cups chopped walnuts
Buttery Rum Sauce
      (recipe follows)

Buttery Rum Sauce
Makes about 1 cup
¾   cup granulated sugar
6   tablespoons unsalted
      butter
3   tablespoons spiced rum
3   tablespoons water
½   cup chopped walnuts

Cake: In a small saucepan, heat rum over medium heat for 5 minutes. Remove from heat; stir in all raisins. Cover and let stand for 30 minutes.

Spray a 10-inch tube pan with baking spray with flour.

In the bowl of a stand mixer fitted with the paddle attachment, beat butter and sugars at medium speed until creamy, 3 to 4 minutes, stopping to scrape sides of bowl. Add eggs, one at a time, beating well after each addition. Stir in condensed milk, whole milk, and vanilla.

Reduce mixer speed to low. Gradually add flour to butter mixture, beating until combined. Stir in raisin mixture and walnuts. Spoon batter into prepared pan.

Place pan in a cold oven. Bake at 300° until a wooden pick inserted near center comes out clean, 1½ hours to 1 hour and 40 minutes, covering with foil halfway through baking to prevent excess browning, if necessary. Let cool in pan for 10 minutes. Remove from pan, and let cool completely on a wire rack. Spoon Buttery Rum Sauce over cake just before serving.

Buttery Rum Sauce: In a small saucepan, bring sugar, butter, rum, and 3 tablespoons water to a boil over medium heat. Boil for 3 minutes; remove from heat, and stir in walnuts.

Fresh Peach Pound Cake

1	cup unsalted butter, softened
3	cups sugar
6	large eggs
1	teaspoon vanilla extract
¼	teaspoon rum extract
½	cup sour cream
1	(3-ounce) box peach gelatin
3	cups all-purpose flour
½	teaspoon salt
¼	teaspoon baking soda
¼	teaspoon ground cinnamon
⅛	teaspoon ground nutmeg
2	cups chopped fresh peaches

Preheat oven to 325°. Spray a 10-inch tube pan with baking spray with flour.

In a large bowl, beat butter and sugar with a mixer at medium speed until fluffy, 3 to 4 minutes, stopping to scrape sides of bowl. Add eggs, one at a time, beating well after each addition. Stir in extracts.

In a small bowl, combine sour cream and gelatin. Set aside.

In another large bowl, whisk together flour, salt, baking soda, cinnamon, and nutmeg. Reduce mixer speed to low. Gradually add flour mixture to butter mixture, beating until combined. Fold in sour cream mixture and peaches. Spoon batter into prepared pan.

Bake for 1 hour. Cover loosely with foil, and bake until a wooden pick inserted near center comes out clean, 40 to 50 minutes more. Let cool in pan for 10 minutes. Remove from pan, and let cool completely on a wire rack.

Chocolate Amaretto Pound Cake

Cake

- 1½ cups unsalted butter, softened
- 3   cups sugar
- 5   large eggs
- ¼   cup almond liqueur
- 2   cups all-purpose flour
- ¾   cup unsweetened cocoa powder
- ½   teaspoon salt
- ½   teaspoon baking powder
- 1   cup semisweet chocolate morsels
- 1   cup sour cream
- Chocolate Amaretto Glaze (recipe follows)
- Candied Almonds (recipe follows)

Chocolate Amaretto Glaze
Makes about ¾ cup

- 1   (4-ounce) bar semisweet chocolate, chopped
- ¼   cup heavy whipping cream
- 2   tablespoons almond liqueur

Candied Almonds
Makes about 1 cup

- 1   cup slivered almonds
- 6   tablespoons sugar
- 1   teaspoon salt

Spray a 10-inch tube pan with baking spray with flour.

Cake: In the bowl of a stand mixer fitted with the paddle attachment, beat butter and sugar at medium speed until fluffy, 3 to 4 minutes, stopping to scrape sides of bowl. Add eggs, one at a time, beating well after each addition. Beat in liqueur.

In a large bowl, whisk together flour, cocoa, salt, and baking powder. Reduce mixer speed to low. Gradually add flour mixture to butter mixture, beating until combined. Stir in chocolate morsels and sour cream. Spoon batter into prepared pan.

Place pan in a cold oven. Bake at 325° until a wooden pick inserted near center comes out clean, 1 hour and 20 minutes to 1½ hours, covering with foil halfway through baking to prevent excess browning, if necessary. Let cool in pan for 10 minutes. Remove from pan, and let cool completely on a wire rack. Drizzle with Chocolate Amaretto Glaze, and sprinkle with Candied Almonds before serving.

Chocolate Amaretto Glaze: In a small saucepan, combine chocolate, cream, and liqueur. Cook over medium-low heat, stirring frequently, until chocolate is melted and mixture is smooth.

Candied Almonds: In a large skillet, stir together almonds and sugar. Cook over medium heat, stirring constantly, until sugar is melted and almonds are browned. Spread in a single layer on parchment paper; sprinkle with salt. Let stand until cool, about 30 minutes. Store in an airtight container for up to 2 weeks.

Black Forest
Pound Cake

Cake
1½ cups unsalted butter,
    softened
1½ cups granulated sugar
1   cup firmly packed brown
    sugar
5   large eggs
1   tablespoon vanilla extract
3   cups all-purpose flour
¼   cup Dutch process cocoa
    powder
1   teaspoon baking powder
½   teaspoon salt
2   (4-ounce) bars semisweet
    chocolate, chopped
1   cup heavy whipping cream
1   cup sour cream
Chocolate Glaze
    (recipe follows)
Brandied Cherry Sauce
    (recipe follows)

Chocolate Glaze
Makes about ¾ cup
1   (4-ounce) bar semisweet
    chocolate, chopped
⅓   cup heavy whipping cream

Brandied Cherry Sauce
Makes about 4 cups
2   (12-ounce) packages frozen
    cherries
⅓   cup granulated sugar
⅓   cup cold water
2   tablespoons cornstarch
2   tablespoons brandy

Spray a 10-inch tube pan with baking spray with flour.

Cake: In the bowl of a stand mixer fitted with the paddle attachment, beat butter and sugars at medium speed until fluffy, 3 to 4 minutes, stopping to scrape sides of bowl. Add eggs, one at a time, beating well after each addition. Beat in vanilla.

In a large bowl, whisk together flour, cocoa, baking powder, and salt. Reduce mixer speed to low. Gradually add flour mixture to butter mixture, beating until combined.

In a small saucepan, combine chocolate and cream. Cook over medium-low heat, stirring frequently, until chocolate is melted and mixture is smooth. Add chocolate mixture to butter mixture, beating until combined. Stir in sour cream. Spoon batter into prepared pan.

Place pan in a cold oven. Bake at 325° until a wooden pick inserted near center comes out clean, 1 hour and 20 minutes to 1½ hours, covering with foil halfway through baking to prevent excess browning, if necessary. Let cool in pan for 10 minutes. Remove from pan, and let cool completely on a wire rack. Drizzle with Chocolate Glaze. Let stand until chocolate is set, about 20 minutes. Spoon Brandied Cherry Sauce over cake just before serving.

Chocolate Glaze: In a small saucepan, combine chocolate and cream. Cook over medium-low heat, stirring frequently, until chocolate is melted and mixture is smooth.

Brandied Cherry Sauce: In a medium saucepan, combine cherries and sugar.

In a small bowl, whisk together ⅓ cup cold water and cornstarch; add to cherry mixture, stirring to combine. Bring to a boil over medium heat, stirring constantly. Reduce heat, and simmer until mixture is very thick, 5 to 6 minutes. Remove from heat; stir in brandy. Let cool for 15 minutes before serving. Serve warm or cold.

Chocolate Pound Cake

1   cup unsalted butter, softened
½   cup all-vegetable shortening
3   cups sugar
5   large eggs
1   tablespoon vanilla extract
3   cups all-purpose flour
5   tablespoons unsweetened cocoa powder
½   teaspoon baking powder
½   teaspoon baking soda
½   teaspoon salt
1   cup whole buttermilk

Preheat oven to 325°. Spray a 10-inch tube pan with baking spray with flour.

In a large bowl, beat butter, shortening, and sugar with a mixer at medium speed until fluffy, 3 to 4 minutes, stopping to scrape sides of bowl. Add eggs, one at a time, beating well after each addition. Beat in vanilla.

In another large bowl, whisk together flour, cocoa, baking powder, baking soda, and salt. Reduce mixer speed to low. Gradually add flour mixture to butter mixture alternately with buttermilk, beginning and ending with flour mixture, beating just until combined after each addition. Spread batter into prepared pan.

Bake until a wooden pick inserted near center comes out clean, 1 hour and 30 minutes to 1 hour and 45 minutes. Let cool in pan for 15 minutes. Remove from pan, and let cool completely on a wire rack. Store in an airtight container for up to 3 days.

cake tip

Whisking together the dry ingredients distributes the leaveners evenly throughout the cake batter, resulting in a good, even rise.

Cinnamon and Chocolate Swirl Pound Cake

1 (4-ounce) bar semisweet chocolate, chopped
⅓ cup confectioners' sugar
⅓ cup heavy whipping cream
1 tablespoon unsalted butter
1 tablespoon light corn syrup
1½ cups butter-flavored shortening
3 cups granulated sugar
1 tablespoon ground cinnamon
5 large eggs, room temperature
3 cups all-purpose flour
½ teaspoon salt
½ teaspoon baking powder
1 cup whole buttermilk, room temperature
1 teaspoon vanilla extract

Preheat oven to 325°. Spray a 10-inch tube pan with baking spray with flour.

In a small bowl, place chocolate. In a small saucepan, bring confectioners' sugar, cream, butter, and corn syrup to a boil over medium-high heat. Pour hot cream mixture over chopped chocolate, whisking until smooth. Set aside.

In a large bowl, beat shortening, granulated sugar, and cinnamon with a mixer at medium speed until fluffy, 3 to 4 minutes, stopping to scrape sides of bowl. Reduce mixer speed to medium. Add eggs, one at a time, beating well after each addition.

In a medium bowl, sift together flour, salt, and baking powder. In a small bowl, combine buttermilk and vanilla. Reduce mixer speed to low. Gradually add flour mixture to shortening mixture alternately with buttermilk mixture, beginning and ending with flour mixture, beating just until combined after each addition. Pour half of batter into prepared pan. Pour chocolate mixture over batter. Using a knife, swirl chocolate mixture through batter. Pour remaining batter over chocolate mixture. Tap pan on counter to release any air bubbles.

Bake for 45 minutes. Cover with foil, and bake until a wooden pick inserted near center comes out clean, about 45 minutes more. Let cool in pan for 20 minutes. Remove from pan, and let cool completely on a wire rack. Store in an airtight container at room temperature.

Cinnamon-Orange Pound Cake

MAKES 10 TO 12 SERVINGS

¾ cup unsalted butter, softened
¾ cup all-vegetable shortening
3 cups granulated sugar
2 tablespoons orange zest
7 large eggs
1½ teaspoons vanilla extract
3 cups all-purpose flour
2 teaspoons ground cinnamon
¼ teaspoon salt
¾ cup whole milk
Garnish: sifted confectioners' sugar, candied orange slices

Preheat oven to 300°. Spray a 12-cup tube pan with baking spray with flour. Line pan with parchment paper.

In a large bowl, beat butter, shortening, granulated sugar, and zest with a mixer at medium speed until fluffy, 3 to 4 minutes, stopping to scrape sides of bowl. Add eggs, one at a time, beating well after each addition. Beat in vanilla.

In a medium bowl, sift together flour, cinnamon, and salt. Reduce mixer speed to low. Gradually add flour mixture to butter mixture alternately with milk, beginning and ending with flour mixture, beating just until combined after each addition. Spoon batter into prepared pan.

Bake for 1 hour. Cover loosely with foil, and bake until a wooden pick inserted near center comes out clean, 45 to 50 minutes more. Let cool in pan for 15 minutes. Remove from pan, and let cool completely on a wire rack. Garnish with confectioners' sugar and candied orange slices, if desired.

Note: Make candied orange slices at home or look for them at your local gourmet food store.

Browned Butter and Spiced Pear Cake

2 tablespoons unsalted butter, softened
¼ cup all-purpose flour

Browned Butter
¾ cup unsalted butter

Cake
2 tablespoons unsalted butter
3 cups thinly sliced peeled Bosc pears (about 3 pears)
1¼ teaspoons ground cinnamon, divided
1½ cups sugar
3 large eggs
3 cups all-purpose flour
1½ teaspoons baking powder
¾ teaspoon baking soda
¾ teaspoon salt
¼ teaspoon ground ginger
¼ teaspoon ground nutmeg
¼ teaspoon ground allspice
1¼ cups whole buttermilk
1½ teaspoons vanilla extract

Topping
¼ cup sugar

Preheat oven to 300°. Lightly coat a 10-inch tube pan with butter. Sprinkle with flour, rotating to coat bottom and sides of pan. Using a pastry brush, remove excess flour.

Browned butter: In a medium saucepan, melt butter over medium heat. Cook until butter turns a medium-brown color and has a nutty aroma, about 10 minutes. Remove from heat, and let cool to room temperature. Refrigerate, stirring occasionally, until almost firm, about 1 hour.

Cake: In a large skillet, melt butter over medium-high heat. Add pears and ¼ teaspoon cinnamon; cook, turning occasionally, until lightly browned and tender, about 5 minutes. Remove from heat, and let cool completely.

In a large bowl, beat browned butter and sugar with a mixer at medium speed until fluffy, 3 to 4 minutes, stopping to scrape sides of bowl. Add eggs, one at a time, beating well after each addition.

In a medium bowl, whisk together flour, baking powder, baking soda, salt, ginger, nutmeg, allspice, and remaining 1 teaspoon cinnamon. Reduce mixer speed to low. Gradually add flour mixture to butter mixture alternately with buttermilk, beginning and ending with flour mixture, beating just until combined after each addition. Fold in pears and vanilla. Spoon batter into prepared pan, smoothing top using an offset spatula. Tap pan twice on counter to release any air bubbles.

Bake until a wooden pick inserted near center comes out clean, about 1 hour and 5 minutes. Let cool in pan for 10 minutes. Invert onto a wire rack. Place a serving plate on cake, and turn flat side up. Sprinkle warm cake with sugar. Let cool completely.

Filled with fall spices and coated with granulated sugar, this cake tastes just like a doughnut.

Tres Leches Pound Cake

2 cups unsalted butter, softened
3 cups plus 2 tablespoons granulated sugar, divided
6 large eggs
4½ cups all-purpose flour
½ teaspoon salt
1 (14-ounce) can sweetened condensed milk
½ cup whole milk
3 teaspoons vanilla extract, divided
¼ cup water
1 cup heavy whipping cream
Garnish: confectioners' sugar

Preheat oven to 300°. Spray a 15-cup tube pan with baking spray with flour.

In the bowl of a stand mixer fitted with the paddle attachment, beat butter and 2 cups granulated sugar at medium speed until creamy, 3 to 4 minutes, stopping to scrape sides of bowl. Add eggs, one at a time, beating well after each addition.

In a medium bowl, whisk together flour and salt. In another medium bowl, whisk together condensed milk, milk, and 2 teaspoons vanilla. Reduce mixer speed to low. Gradually add flour mixture to butter mixture alternately with milk mixture, beginning and ending with flour mixture, beating just until combined after each addition. Pour batter into prepared pan.

Bake until a wooden pick inserted near center comes out clean, about 1½ hours.

In a small saucepan, bring ¼ cup water and remaining 1 cup and 2 tablespoons granulated sugar to a boil over medium-high heat. Remove from heat. Gradually whisk in cream and remaining 1 teaspoon vanilla. Let cool completely.

Using a wooden pick or skewer, poke holes in warm cake in pan. Slowly pour 1 cup cream mixture over top of cake in pan. Let cool for 30 minutes. Invert cake onto a wire rack lined with foil. Poke holes in cake, and pour remaining cream mixture over cake. Let cool completely. Invert onto a serving plate, and drizzle with remaining cream mixture in foil. Garnish with confectioners' sugar, if desired.

bundt cakes

Scalloped pans give a fancy, fluted look to
pound cakes. The shape offers a suggestion of each slice
width, making it a popular choice among hosts.

Sour Cream Pound Cake

1¼ cups unsalted butter, softened

3 cups sugar

6 large eggs

1 vanilla bean, split lengthwise, seeds scraped and reserved

1 tablespoon vanilla extract

3 cups all-purpose flour

½ teaspoon baking soda

¼ teaspoon salt

1 (8-ounce) container sour cream

Garnish: fresh raspberries, whipped cream

Preheat oven to 325°. Spray a 12-cup Bundt pan with baking spray with flour.

In a large bowl, beat butter and sugar with a mixer at medium speed until fluffy, 3 to 4 minutes, stopping to scrape sides of bowl. Add eggs, one at a time, beating well after each addition. Beat in reserved vanilla bean seeds and vanilla extract.

In a medium bowl, whisk together flour, baking soda, and salt. Reduce mixer speed to low. Gradually add flour mixture to butter mixture, beating just until combined. Stir in sour cream. Spoon batter into prepared pan.

Bake until a wooden pick inserted near center comes out clean, about 1 hour, covering with foil to prevent excess browning, if necessary. Let cool in pan for 10 minutes. Remove from pan, and let cool completely on a wire rack. Garnish with raspberries and whipped cream, if desired.

Almond–Sour Cream Bundt Cake

MAKES ABOUT 16 SERVINGS

1½ cups unsalted butter, softened
3   cups granulated sugar
6   large eggs
1   teaspoon vanilla extract
3   cups all-purpose flour
½   cup finely ground almonds
1   teaspoon lemon zest
½   teaspoon baking soda
1   (8-ounce) container sour cream
Garnish: confectioners' sugar

Preheat oven to 325°. Spray a 10- to 15-cup Bundt pan with baking spray with flour.

In a large bowl, beat butter and granulated sugar with a mixer at medium speed until fluffy, 3 to 4 minutes, stopping to scrape sides of bowl. Add eggs, one at a time, beating well after each addition. Beat in vanilla.

In a medium bowl, combine flour, almonds, zest, and baking soda. Reduce mixer speed to low. Gradually add flour mixture to butter mixture alternately with sour cream, beginning and ending with flour mixture, beating just until combined after each addition. Spoon batter into prepared pan.

Bake until a wooden pick inserted near center comes out clean, 1 hour to 1 hour and 15 minutes. Let cool in pan for 10 minutes. Remove from pan, and let cool completely on a wire rack. Garnish with confectioners' sugar, if desired.

Delta Pound Cake

MAKES ABOUT 16 SERVINGS

1½ cups unsalted butter,
    softened
3   cups granulated sugar
7   large eggs
3   cups all-purpose flour
¼   teaspoon salt
1   cup heavy whipping cream
1½ teaspoons vanilla extract
Garnish: sifted confectioners'
    sugar

Preheat oven to 300°. Spray a 10- to 15-cup Bundt pan with baking spray with flour.

In a large bowl, beat butter and granulated sugar with a mixer at medium speed until fluffy, 3 to 4 minutes, stopping to scrape sides of bowl. Add eggs, one at a time, beating well after each addition.

In a medium bowl, sift together flour and salt. Reduce mixer speed to low. Gradually add flour mixture to butter mixture alternately with cream, beginning and ending with flour mixture, beating just until combined after each addition. Beat in vanilla. Spoon batter into prepared pan.

Bake for 1 hour. Cover loosely with foil, and bake until a wooden pick inserted near center comes out clean, 45 to 55 minutes more. Let cool in pan for 15 minutes. Remove from pan, and let cool completely on a wire rack. Garnish with confectioners' sugar, if desired.

Citrus Pound Cake,
page 58.

Lemonade Pound Cake

MAKES 12 SERVINGS

Cake
1½ cups unsalted butter,
    softened
2   cups granulated sugar
5   large eggs
3   cups all-purpose flour
1   teaspoon baking soda
1   teaspoon salt
¾   cup frozen lemonade
    concentrate, thawed
½   cup sour cream
2   tablespoons lemon zest
Lemonade Glaze
    (recipe follows)
Garnish: fresh lemon slices,
    fresh mint

Lemonade Glaze
Makes about 1 cup
¼   cup heavy whipping cream
2   tablespoons frozen
    lemonade concentrate,
    thawed
2   cups confectioners' sugar

Preheat oven to 325°. Spray a 15-cup Bundt pan with baking spray with flour.

Cake: In a large bowl, beat butter and sugar with a mixer at medium speed until fluffy, 3 to 4 minutes, stopping to scrape sides of bowl. Add eggs, one at a time, beating well after each addition.

In a medium bowl, whisk together flour, baking soda, and salt. Reduce mixer speed to low. Gradually add flour mixture to butter mixture alternately with lemonade and sour cream, beginning and ending with flour mixture, beating just until combined after each addition. Add zest, beating to combine. Pour batter into prepared pan.

Bake until a wooden pick inserted near center comes out clean, about 1 hour. Let cool in pan for 10 minutes. Remove from pan, and let cool completely on a wire rack. Drizzle with Lemonade Glaze. Garnish with lemon slices and mint, if desired.

Lemonade Glaze: In a medium bowl, combine cream and lemonade concentrate. Gradually whisk in confectioners' sugar until smooth.

Citrus Pound Cake

Cake
1   cup unsalted butter,
    softened
3   cups granulated sugar
6   large eggs
3   cups all-purpose flour
½   teaspoon baking soda
1½ teaspoons lemon zest
1½ teaspoons lime zest
1½ teaspoons orange zest
1   cup sour cream
2   tablespoons fresh lemon
    juice
2   tablespoons fresh lime
    juice
2   tablespoons fresh orange
    juice
Citrus Glaze (recipe follows)

Citrus Glaze
Makes about 1 cup
2   cups confectioners' sugar
½   teaspoon lemon zest
½   teaspoon lime zest
½   teaspoon orange zest
¼   cup fresh orange juice

Preheat oven to 325°. Spray a 10-cup Bundt pan with baking spray with flour.

Cake: In a large bowl, beat butter and sugar with a mixer at medium speed until fluffy, 3 to 4 minutes, stopping to scrape sides of bowl. Add eggs, one at a time, beating well after each addition.

In a medium bowl, whisk together flour, baking soda, and zests. Reduce mixer speed to low. Gradually add flour mixture to butter mixture, beating just until combined. Add sour cream and juices, beating until combined. Spoon batter into prepared pan.

Bake until a wooden pick inserted near center comes out clean, 1 hour and 5 minutes to 1 hour and 10 minutes. Let cool in pan for 10 minutes. Remove from pan, and let cool completely on a wire rack. Drizzle with Citrus Glaze.

Citrus Glaze: In a small bowl, whisk together all ingredients until combined. Use immediately.

Lime Buttermilk Bundt Cake

MAKES 10 TO 12 SERVINGS

Cake
3   cups all-purpose flour
1½   teaspoons salt
1   teaspoon baking powder
½   teaspoon baking soda
1½   cups unsalted butter,
     softened
2   cups granulated sugar
3   large eggs, separated
1½   cups whole buttermilk
1   teaspoon vanilla extract
1   tablespoon lime zest (from
     about 2 limes)
¼   cup plus additional Lime
     Syrup (recipe follows)

Lime Syrup
Makes about ¾ cup
½   cup granulated sugar
2   tablespoons lime zest
     (from about 4 limes)
½   cup fresh lime juice

Glaze
2   cups confectioners' sugar
½   cup Lime Syrup
     (recipe follows)

Garnish: lime zest

Preheat oven to 325°. Spray a 15-cup Bundt pan with baking spray with flour.

Cake: In a medium bowl, whisk together flour, salt, baking powder, and baking soda. Set aside.

In a large bowl, beat butter and sugar with a mixer at medium speed until fluffy, 3 to 4 minutes, stopping to scrape sides of bowl. Add egg yolks, one at a time, beating well after each addition. Reduce mixer speed to low. Gradually add flour mixture to butter mixture alternately with buttermilk, beginning and ending with flour mixture, beating just until combined after each addition. Beat in vanilla and lime zest.

In a medium bowl, beat egg whites with a mixer at medium speed until stiff peaks form. Gently fold egg whites into batter; pour batter into prepared pan.

Bake until a wooden pick inserted near center comes out clean, about 1 hour and 10 minutes. Using a wooden pick, poke holes in bottom of cake. Pour ¼ cup Lime Syrup over warm cake; let stand for 10 minutes. Invert cake onto a wire rack. Brush top of cake with about 1 tablespoon Lime Syrup.

Lime Syrup: In a small bowl, whisk together sugar and lime zest and juice until sugar is dissolved.

Glaze: In a small bowl, whisk together confectioners' sugar and Lime Syrup until smooth; drizzle over cooled cake. Garnish with lime zest, if desired.

Italian Cream Bundt Cake

MAKES 10 TO 12 SERVINGS

1½   cups unsalted butter, softened
1   (8-ounce) package cream cheese, softened
2   cups granulated sugar
1   cup firmly packed light brown sugar
5   large eggs
1   tablespoon vanilla extract
3   cups all-purpose flour
1½   teaspoons salt
½   teaspoon baking powder
1   cup finely chopped pecans, toasted
¾   cup sweetened flaked coconut, toasted
Garnish: confectioners' sugar

Spray a 15-cup Bundt pan with baking spray with flour.

In a large bowl, beat butter, cream cheese, and sugars with a mixer at medium-high speed until fluffy, 3 to 4 minutes, stopping to scrape sides of bowl. Add eggs, one at a time, beating well after each addition. Beat in vanilla.

In a medium bowl, whisk together flour, salt, and baking powder. Reduce mixer speed to low. Gradually add flour mixture to butter mixture, beating just until combined. Stir in pecans and coconut. Spoon batter into prepared pan.

Place pan in a cold oven. Bake at 300° until a wooden pick inserted near center comes out clean, about 1 hour and 20 minutes. Let cool in pan for 10 minutes. Remove from pan, and let cool completely on a wire rack. Garnish with confectioners' sugar, if desired.

White Chocolate Pound Cake

1 cup unsalted butter, softened
2 cups granulated sugar
5 large eggs
3 cups all-purpose flour
½ teaspoon baking soda
½ teaspoon baking powder
½ teaspoon salt
1 cup whole buttermilk
2 (4-ounce) bars white chocolate, melted
Garnish: confectioners' sugar

Preheat oven to 300°. Spray a 10-cup Bundt pan with baking spray with flour.

In a large bowl, beat butter and sugar with a mixer at medium speed until fluffy, 3 to 4 minutes, stopping to scrape sides of bowl. Add eggs, one at a time, beating well after each addition.

In another large bowl, whisk together flour, baking soda, baking powder, and salt. Reduce mixer speed to low. Gradually add flour mixture to butter mixture alternately with buttermilk, beginning and ending with flour mixture, beating just until combined after each addition. Stir in melted chocolate. Spoon batter into prepared pan.

Bake until a wooden pick inserted near center comes out clean, about 1½ hours. Let cool in pan for 10 minutes. Remove from pan, and let cool completely on a wire rack. Garnish with confectioners' sugar, if desired.

Almond-Topped Sour Cream Pound Cake

MAKES 10 TO 12 SERVINGS

Cake
- ¼ cup sliced almonds
- 1½ cups unsalted butter, softened
- 1 cup granulated sugar
- 6 large eggs
- 3 cups all-purpose flour
- ⅛ teaspoon baking soda
- 1 (8-ounce) container sour cream
- 2 teaspoons almond extract
- 1 teaspoon vanilla extract

Sour Cream Topping
- 1 cup sour cream
- 1 cup confectioners' sugar
- 1 teaspoon vanilla extract

Preheat oven to 325°. Spray a 15-cup Bundt pan with baking spray with flour.

Cake: Sprinkle sliced almonds into bottom of prepared pan. In a large bowl, beat butter and sugar with a mixer at medium speed until creamy, 3 to 4 minutes, stopping to scrape sides of bowl. Add eggs, one at a time, beating well after each addition.

In a medium bowl, whisk together flour and baking soda. Reduce mixer speed to low. Gradually add flour mixture to butter mixture alternately with sour cream, beginning and ending with flour mixture, beating just until combined after each addition. Beat in extracts. Pour batter into prepared pan.

Bake until lightly browned and a wooden pick inserted near center comes out clean, 1 hour and 10 minutes to 1 hour and 20 minutes. Let cool in pan for 10 minutes. Invert onto a serving plate, and let cool completely. Serve with Sour Cream Topping.

Sour Cream Topping: In a small bowl, stir together sour cream, confectioners' sugar, and vanilla.

Banana-Coconut Pound Cake

MAKES ABOUT 16 SERVINGS

Cake
1½	cups unsalted butter, softened
3	cups granulated sugar
6	large eggs
3	cups all-purpose flour
1½	teaspoons baking powder
1	teaspoon salt
¾	cup whole milk
1½	cups mashed ripe banana
1	cup sweetened flaked coconut
1	cup chopped walnuts
1	tablespoon vanilla extract

Banana Glaze (recipe follows)

Banana Glaze
Makes about 1 cup
2	cups confectioners' sugar
¼	cup whole milk
¼	teaspoon banana extract

Preheat oven to 350°. Spray a 10- to 15-cup Bundt pan with baking spray with flour.

Cake: In a large bowl, beat butter and sugar with a mixer at medium speed until fluffy, 3 to 4 minutes, stopping to scrape sides of bowl. Add eggs, one at a time, beating well after each addition.

In a medium bowl, whisk together flour, baking powder, and salt. Reduce mixer speed to low. Gradually add flour mixture to butter mixture alternately with milk, beginning and ending with flour mixture, beating just until combined after each addition. Add mashed banana, coconut, walnuts, and vanilla, beating until combined. Spoon batter into prepared pan.

Bake until a wooden pick inserted near center comes out clean, 1 hour and 35 minutes to 1 hour and 40 minutes. Let cool in pan for 10 minutes. Remove from pan, and let cool completely on a wire rack. Drizzle with Banana Glaze.

Banana Glaze: In a small bowl, whisk together all ingredients until smooth. Use immediately.

Orange Pound Cake

MAKES 10 TO 12 SERVINGS

Cream Cheese Swirl
1   (8-ounce) package cream
    cheese, softened
½   cup confectioners' sugar
2   tablespoons all-purpose
    flour
1   large egg
1   teaspoon orange zest

Cake
1½ cups unsalted butter,
    softened
1   (8-ounce) package cream
    cheese, softened
3   cups granulated sugar
2   tablespoons orange zest
6   large eggs
1   teaspoon vanilla extract
3   cups all-purpose flour
½   cup whole milk
½   cup chopped pecans,
    toasted

Glaze
2   cups confectioners' sugar,
    sifted
2   tablespoons fresh orange
    juice

Garnish: orange slices

Preheat oven to 325°. Spray a 15-cup Bundt pan with baking spray with flour.

Cream Cheese Swirl: In a medium bowl, beat cream cheese with a mixer at medium speed until creamy, about 3 minutes. Add confectioners' sugar, flour, egg, and zest, beating until smooth, about 2 minutes. Cover and refrigerate until ready to use.

Cake: In the bowl of a stand mixer fitted with the paddle attachment, beat butter and cream cheese at medium speed until creamy, about 3 minutes. Add sugar and zest, and beat until fluffy, about 2 minutes. Add eggs, one at a time, beating well after each addition. Beat in vanilla.

Reduce mixer speed to low. Gradually add flour to butter mixture alternately with milk, beginning and ending with flour, beating just until combined after each addition. Stir in pecans.

Spoon half of batter into prepared pan. Spoon Cream Cheese Swirl onto batter, avoiding edges of pan. Top with remaining batter. Using a knife, pull blade back and forth through batter to swirl layers together. Smooth top with an offset spatula.

Bake until a wooden pick inserted near center comes out clean, about 1½ hours. Let cool in pan for 10 minutes. Remove from pan, and let cool completely on a wire rack.

Glaze: In a small bowl, whisk together confectioners' sugar and orange juice until smooth. Drizzle over cooled cake. Garnish with orange slices, if desired.

This cake is a beautiful
blend of sweet cornbread and
buttermilk pound cake.

Vanilla Bean Pound Cake with Honey-Orange Drizzle

MAKES ABOUT 8 SERVINGS

2   tablespoons unsalted butter, softened
¼   cup all-purpose flour

Cake
1   cup unsalted butter, softened
1   cup sugar
1   vanilla bean, split lengthwise, seeds scraped and reserved
3   large eggs
1   cup all-purpose flour
¼   cup stone-ground yellow cornmeal
½   teaspoon baking powder
¼   teaspoon salt
⅓   cup whole buttermilk
3   tablespoons honey
½   teaspoon orange zest
Garnish: star anise

Honey-Orange Drizzle
½   cup honey
4   (2-inch) strips orange zest
2   tablespoons fresh orange juice
2   star anise
2   cinnamon sticks

Preheat oven to 300°. Lightly coat a 6-cup Bundt pan with butter. Sprinkle with flour, rotating to coat bottom and sides of pan. Using a pastry brush, remove excess flour.

Cake: In a large bowl, beat butter, sugar, and reserved vanilla bean seeds with a mixer at medium speed until creamy, 3 to 4 minutes, stopping to scrape sides of bowl. Add eggs, one at a time, beating well after each addition.

In a medium bowl, whisk together flour, cornmeal, baking powder, and salt. Reduce mixer speed to low. Gradually add flour mixture to butter mixture, beating until combined. Beat in buttermilk, honey, and zest. Spoon batter into prepared pan, smoothing top using an offset spatula.

Bake until a wooden pick inserted near center comes out clean, about 1 hour. Let cool in pan for 10 minutes. Remove from pan, and let cool completely on a wire rack. Pour Honey-Orange Drizzle over cake. Garnish with star anise, if desired.

Honey-Orange Drizzle: In a small saucepan, combine honey, orange zest and juice, star anise, and cinnamon. Cook over low heat until warm, about 15 minutes.

Strawberry Swirl Pound Cake

MAKES ABOUT 10 SERVINGS

Cake
- 2 tablespoons cool water
- 1 tablespoon cornstarch
- 1 cup puréed fresh strawberries
- 3 cups plus 3 tablespoons granulated sugar, divided
- 1 cup unsalted butter, softened
- 1 (8-ounce) package cream cheese, softened
- 6 large eggs
- 1 tablespoon orange zest
- 1 tablespoon vanilla extract
- 3½ cups all-purpose flour
- 1 teaspoon baking powder
- 1 teaspoon salt
- 1 cup heavy whipping cream
- Buttermilk-Orange Glaze (recipe follows)
- Garnish: fresh strawberries, fresh mint

Buttermilk-Orange Glaze
Makes about ½ cup
- 1½ cups confectioners' sugar
- 2 tablespoons whole buttermilk
- 1 tablespoon orange liqueur

Preheat oven to 325°. Spray a 12- to 15-cup Bundt pan with baking spray with flour.

Cake: In a small bowl, whisk together 2 tablespoons cool water and cornstarch until smooth.

In a small saucepan, stir together cornstarch mixture, strawberry purée, and 3 tablespoons sugar. Bring to a boil over medium-high heat, stirring frequently; boil until mixture is thickened, about 1 minute. Remove from heat, and let cool completely. Set aside.

In a large bowl, beat butter and remaining 3 cups sugar with a mixer at medium speed until fluffy, 3 to 4 minutes, stopping to scrape sides of bowl. Add cream cheese, beating until smooth. Add eggs, one at a time, beating well after each addition. Beat in zest and vanilla.

In a medium bowl, whisk together flour, baking powder, and salt. Reduce mixer speed to low. Gradually add flour mixture to butter mixture alternately with cream, beginning and ending with flour mixture, beating just until combined after each addition.

Spoon one-third of batter into prepared pan. Spoon half of strawberry mixture over batter. Repeat layers, ending with batter. Using a knife, gently swirl layers.

Bake until a wooden pick inserted near center comes out clean, about 1 hour and 15 minutes, covering with foil halfway through baking to prevent excess browning. Let cool in pan for 10 minutes. Remove from pan, and let cool completely on a wire rack. Spoon Buttermilk-Orange Glaze over cake, and garnish with strawberries and mint, if desired. Store covered at room temperature for up to 5 days.

Buttermilk-Orange Glaze: In a small bowl, whisk together all ingredients until smooth. Whisk in additional confectioners' sugar if a thicker consistency is desired. Use immediately.

Cranberry Swirl Bundt Cake

MAKES ABOUT 10 SERVINGS

Cake

1½	cups unsalted butter, softened
1	cup sour cream
3	cups granulated sugar
5	large eggs
1	egg yolk
1	tablespoon orange zest
1	teaspoon vanilla extract
3¼	cups all-purpose flour
1	teaspoon apple pie spice
½	teaspoon baking soda
¼	teaspoon salt
½	cup Whole-Berry Cranberry Sauce (recipe follows)

Glaze

6	tablespoons heavy whipping cream
½	teaspoon vanilla extract
1¼	cups confectioners' sugar

Whole-Berry Cranberry Sauce
Makes about 3½ cups

2	(12-ounce) packages fresh cranberries
1¾	cups firmly packed brown sugar
1	cup orange juice
½	cup water
1	teaspoon minced fresh ginger
½	teaspoon vanilla extract

Preheat oven to 325°. Spray a 12- to 15-cup Bundt pan with baking spray with flour.

Cake: In a large bowl, beat butter and sour cream with a mixer at medium speed until creamy. Add sugar, beating until fluffy, 3 to 4 minutes, stopping to scrape sides of bowl. Add eggs and egg yolk, one at a time, beating well after each addition. Add zest and vanilla, beating until combined.

In a medium bowl, whisk together flour, apple pie spice, baking soda, and salt. Reduce mixer speed to low. Gradually add flour mixture to butter mixture, beating just until combined. Reserve 2 cups batter in a medium bowl. Add Whole-Berry Cranberry Sauce to reserved batter, and stir until combined. Spoon 3 cups plain batter into prepared pan. Add cranberry batter. Top with remaining plain batter. Run a knife through batter 8 times to swirl filling slightly. Gently tap pan on counter to release any air bubbles.

Bake until a wooden pick inserted near center comes out clean, about 1 hour and 15 minutes, covering with foil halfway through baking to prevent excess browning, if necessary. Let cool in pan for 10 minutes. Remove from pan, and let cool completely on a wire rack. Drizzle cake with Glaze.

Glaze: In a small bowl, whisk together cream and vanilla. Add confectioners' sugar, whisking until smooth.

Whole-Berry Cranberry Sauce: In a medium saucepan, bring all ingredients to a boil over medium-high heat. Reduce heat, and simmer, stirring occasionally, until berries burst and sauce thickens, 25 to 30 minutes. Store in an airtight container in refrigerator for up to 3 days, or freeze in an airtight container for up to 2 months.

Vanilla Bundt Cake with Caramel Sauce

Cake

1½	cups unsalted butter, softened
2	cups granulated sugar
1	cup firmly packed dark brown sugar
5	large eggs
3	cups all-purpose flour
1	teaspoon baking powder
½	teaspoon salt
1	cup whole milk
1	tablespoon vanilla extract

Vanilla-Bourbon Caramel Sauce (recipe follows)

Vanilla-Bourbon Caramel Sauce

Makes about 2 cups

2	cups granulated sugar
¼	cup water
½	cup heavy whipping cream
2	tablespoons bourbon
1	teaspoon salt
½	teaspoon vanilla extract

Preheat oven to 325°. Spray a 10- to 15-cup Bundt pan with baking spray with flour.

Cake: In a large bowl, beat butter and sugars with a mixer at medium speed until fluffy, 3 to 4 minutes, stopping to scrape sides of bowl. Add eggs, one at a time, beating well after each addition.

In another large bowl, whisk together flour, baking powder, and salt. Reduce mixer speed to low. Gradually add flour mixture to butter mixture alternately with milk, beginning and ending with flour mixture, beating just until combined after each addition. Beat in vanilla. Spoon batter into prepared pan, smoothing top using an offset spatula. Tap pan on counter twice to release air bubbles.

Bake until a wooden pick inserted near center comes out clean, about 1 hour and 5 minutes. Let cool in pan for 10 minutes. Remove from pan, and let cool completely on a wire rack. Place cake on a serving plate. Drizzle with Vanilla-Bourbon Caramel Sauce.

Vanilla-Bourbon Caramel Sauce: In a medium saucepan, place sugar and ¼ cup water, swirling to combine thoroughly. Cook over medium-high heat, without stirring, until mixture is amber colored, about 10 minutes. Remove from heat. Carefully stir in cream. Stir in bourbon, salt, and vanilla. Let cool in pan for 10 minutes, stirring frequently. Cover and refrigerate for up to 3 weeks.

Fresh Apple Cake with Orange-Cream Cheese Swirl and Caramel Glaze

MAKES 12 TO 16 SERVINGS

Cake

- 2¼ cups peeled, cored, and grated Granny Smith apples (about 3 small apples)
- 2¼ cups peeled, cored, and diced Granny Smith apples (about 3 small apples)
- 2 teaspoons fresh lemon juice
- 4½ cups all-purpose flour
- 1¼ cups firmly packed light brown sugar
- 1 cup granulated sugar
- 3 teaspoons ground cinnamon
- 1½ teaspoons baking soda
- 1½ teaspoons salt
- 1½ teaspoons ground ginger
- 5 large eggs, lightly beaten
- 1¾ cups canola oil
- 1½ teaspoons vanilla extract

Orange-Cream Cheese Swirl

- 1 (8-ounce) package cream cheese, softened
- ½ cup confectioners' sugar
- 2 tablespoons all-purpose flour
- 1 large egg
- 1 tablespoon orange zest

Caramel Glaze

Makes about 2¼ cups

- 1½ cups granulated sugar
- ½ cup water
- ½ teaspoon fresh lemon juice
- ¾ cup heavy whipping cream
- ¼ cup unsalted butter, softened
- 1 cup confectioners' sugar, sifted

Preheat oven to 325°. Spray a 15-cup Bundt pan with baking spray with flour.

Cake: In a medium bowl, combine apples and lemon juice. Set aside.

In a large bowl, whisk together flour, sugars, cinnamon, baking soda, salt, and ginger. Make a well in center of dry ingredients; add eggs, stirring to combine. (Mixture will be very dry.) Stir in oil. Fold in apples and vanilla.

Orange-Cream Cheese Swirl: In a small bowl, stir together cream cheese, confectioners' sugar, flour, egg, and zest.

Pour half of batter into prepared pan. Spoon cream cheese mixture over batter, avoiding edges of pan. Top with remaining batter. Using a knife, pull blade back and forth through batter to swirl layers. Smooth top with an offset spatula.

Bake until a wooden pick inserted near center comes out clean, about 1 hour and 15 minutes. Let cool in pan for 20 minutes. Remove from pan, and let cool completely on a wire rack. Drizzle with Caramel Glaze.

Caramel Glaze: In a medium saucepan, bring granulated sugar, ½ cup water, and lemon juice to a boil over medium-high heat. Cook, without stirring, until mixture turns light amber colored and registers 340° on a candy thermometer, 10 to 15 minutes. Remove from heat, and carefully whisk in cream and butter. (Mixture will boil vigorously.) Let cool completely. Add confectioners' sugar, whisking until smooth.

Caramel Apple Pound Cake

MAKES 12 TO 16 SERVINGS

Cake

- 1 cup granulated sugar
- 1¼ cups firmly packed light brown sugar, divided
- 1½ cups unsalted butter, melted
- 4 large eggs
- 1 teaspoon vanilla extract
- 3 cups all-purpose flour
- 2 teaspoons baking powder
- 1 teaspoon salt
- 1 teaspoon apple pie spice
- 3 cups chopped Granny Smith apple
- 2 teaspoons ground cinnamon
- Cream Cheese Icing (recipe follows)
- Garnish: chopped walnuts, hot caramel topping*

Cream Cheese Icing
Makes about 2 cups

- 1 (8-ounce) package cream cheese, softened
- 2 cups confectioners' sugar
- ¼ cup whole milk
- ¼ cup hot caramel topping*

Preheat oven to 350°. Spray a 12-cup Bundt pan with baking spray with flour.

Cake: In a large bowl, beat granulated sugar, 1 cup brown sugar, and melted butter with a mixer at medium speed until fluffy, 3 to 4 minutes, stopping to scrape sides of bowl. Add eggs, one at a time, beating well after each addition. Beat in vanilla.

In a medium bowl, whisk together flour, baking powder, salt, and apple pie spice. Reduce mixer speed to low. Gradually add flour mixture to butter mixture, beating just until combined.

In another medium bowl, combine apple, cinnamon, and remaining ¼ cup brown sugar.

Spoon one-third of batter into prepared pan; top with half of apple mixture. Repeat layers once. Top with remaining one-third of batter.

Bake until a wooden pick inserted near center comes out clean, 50 minutes to 1 hour. Let cool in pan for 10 minutes. Remove from pan, and let cool completely on a wire rack. Top with Cream Cheese Icing. Garnish with walnuts and caramel topping, if desired.

Cream Cheese Icing: In a medium bowl, beat cream cheese and confectioners' sugar with a mixer at medium-low speed until smooth. Beat in milk and caramel topping.

*We used Smucker's Hot Caramel Topping.

Pumpkin-Cranberry Bundt Cake

MAKES 8 TO 10 SERVINGS

¾ cup dried cranberries, chopped
½ cup boiling water
2¾ cups self-rising flour
1½ teaspoons pumpkin pie spice
½ cup unsalted butter, softened
½ (8-ounce) package cream cheese, softened
1¾ cups firmly packed light brown sugar
3 large eggs
1 cup canned pumpkin
2 teaspoons vanilla extract
Garnish: confectioners' sugar

Preheat oven to 350°. Spray a 10-cup Bundt pan with baking spray with flour.

In a small bowl, combine cranberries and ½ cup boiling water; let stand for 10 minutes. Drain.

In a medium bowl, whisk together flour and pumpkin pie spice. Set aside.

In a large bowl, beat butter, cream cheese, and brown sugar with a mixer at medium speed until creamy, 3 to 4 minutes, stopping to scrape sides of bowl. Add eggs, one at a time, beating well after each addition.

Reduce mixer speed to low. Gradually add flour mixture to butter mixture, beating until combined. Beat in cranberries, pumpkin, and vanilla. Spoon batter into prepared pan, smoothing top. Tap pan twice on counter to release air bubbles.

Bake until a wooden pick inserted near center comes out clean, about 45 minutes. Let cool in pan for 15 minutes. Remove from pan, and let cool completely on a wire rack. Garnish with confectioners' sugar, if desired.

cake tip

For an extra delightful treat, serve up slices of cake topped with spiced, sweetened whipped cream. In a medium bowl, beat 1 cup heavy whipping cream, 3 tablespoons confectioners' sugar, and ¼ teaspoon pumpkin pie spice with a mixer at high speed until soft peaks form.

*Apple cider is reduced
to give this fresh apple cake
a tart sweet glaze.*

Apple Bundt Cake with Apple Cider Glaze

MAKES ABOUT 12 SERVINGS

2 tablespoons unsalted butter
¼ cup all-purpose flour

Cake
¾ cup plus 2 tablespoons unsalted butter, divided
3 cups chopped peeled Gala apple (about 3 apples)
½ cup apple cider*
1½ cups granulated sugar
3 large eggs
3 cups all-purpose flour
1½ teaspoons baking powder
1½ teaspoons apple pie spice
¾ teaspoon baking soda
¾ teaspoon salt
1¼ cups whole buttermilk
1 teaspoon vanilla extract
⅓ cup chopped toasted pecans

Apple Cider Glaze
¾ cup apple cider*
1½ cups confectioners' sugar
2 tablespoons heavy whipping cream
1 teaspoon unsalted butter, melted
⅛ teaspoon salt

Preheat oven to 300°. Lightly coat a 10- to 15-cup Bundt pan with butter. Sprinkle with flour, rotating to coat bottom and sides of pan. Using a pastry brush, remove excess flour.

Cake: In a large skillet, melt 2 tablespoons butter over medium-high heat. Add apple; cook, stirring occasionally, until lightly browned and tender, about 4 minutes. Add apple cider; cook until liquid is evaporated. Let cool completely.

In a large bowl, beat sugar and remaining ¾ cup butter with a mixer at medium speed until fluffy, 3 to 4 minutes, stopping to scrape sides of bowl. Add eggs, one at a time, beating well after each addition.

In a medium bowl, whisk together flour, baking powder, apple pie spice, baking soda, and salt. Reduce mixer speed to low. Gradually add flour mixture to butter mixture alternately with buttermilk, beginning and ending with flour mixture, beating just until combined after each addition. Fold in apple and vanilla. Spoon batter into prepared pan, smoothing top using an offset spatula. Tap pan twice on counter to release any air bubbles.

Bake until a wooden pick inserted near center comes out clean, about 1 hour. Let cool in pan for 10 minutes. Remove from pan, and let cool completely on a wire rack. Drizzle Apple Cider Glaze over cake; sprinkle with pecans.

Apple Cider Glaze: In a small saucepan, bring cider to a boil over medium-high heat. Boil until cider reduces to ¼ cup, about 7 minutes. Let cool to room temperature. In a medium bowl, whisk together reduced cider, confectioners' sugar, cream, melted butter, and salt until smooth.

*We used Martinelli's Sparkling Cider.

Apple Spice Bundt Cake

Cake
1½   cups unsalted butter, softened
1¾   cups granulated sugar
3   large eggs
3   cups all-purpose flour
1   tablespoon apple pie spice
½   teaspoon salt
½   teaspoon baking powder
½   teaspoon baking soda
3   cups chopped apple, such as Granny Smith or Gala
1   tablespoon vanilla extract
2   teaspoons orange zest
½   cup chopped pecans
Brown Sugar Glaze (recipe follows)
Garnish: Miniature Caramel Apples (see Cake Tip)

Brown Sugar Glaze
Makes about 1 cup
½   cup firmly packed dark brown sugar
3   tablespoons apple cider
2   tablespoons unsalted butter
1   tablespoon dark corn syrup
⅛   teaspoon salt
1   cup confectioners' sugar, sifted

Preheat oven to 325°. Spray a 15-cup Bundt pan with baking spray with flour.

Cake: In a large bowl, beat butter and sugar with a mixer at medium speed until fluffy, 3 to 4 minutes, stopping to scrape sides of bowl. Add eggs, one at a time, beating well after each addition.

In a medium bowl, whisk together flour, apple pie spice, salt, baking powder, and baking soda. Reduce mixer speed to low. Gradually add flour mixture to butter mixture, beating just until combined. Beat in apple, vanilla, and zest. Fold in pecans. (Batter will be thick.) Spoon batter into prepared pan.

Bake until a wooden pick inserted near center comes out clean, about 1 hour and 5 minutes. Let cool in pan for 15 minutes. Remove from pan, and let cool completely on a wire rack. Drizzle with Brown Sugar Glaze. Let stand until glaze is set, about 30 minutes. Garnish with Miniature Caramel Apples, if desired.

Brown Sugar Glaze: In a small saucepan, bring brown sugar, cider, butter, corn syrup, and salt to a boil over medium-high heat. Reduce heat to medium-low; cook for 1 minute. Remove from heat. Add confectioners' sugar; beat with a mixer at low speed for 1 minute. Let cool for 3 minutes before using.

cake tip

To make Miniature Caramel Apples, spray a wire rack with cooking spray. Place rack on a piece of wax paper. Dip Lady apples in Brown Sugar Glaze twice, letting excess drip off. Place on prepared rack, glazed side up. Let stand until set, about 5 minutes.

Apple Butter Pound Cake

Cake

- 1¼ cups firmly packed light brown sugar
- 1 cup apple butter
- ½ cup chopped pecans
- 1½ cups unsalted butter, softened
- 1 (8-ounce) package cream cheese, softened
- 2 cups granulated sugar
- 5 large eggs, room temperature
- 1 tablespoon vanilla extract
- 3 cups all-purpose flour
- 1½ teaspoons salt
- 1 teaspoon ground cinnamon
- ½ teaspoon baking powder
- Glaze (recipe follows)

Glaze
Makes about 2 cups

- 1 cup firmly packed light brown sugar
- ⅔ cup heavy whipping cream
- ½ cup unsalted butter
- 1 teaspoon vanilla extract
- ¼ teaspoon salt
- 1½ cups confectioners' sugar, sifted

Spray a 15-cup Bundt pan with baking spray with flour.

Cake: In a medium bowl, stir together brown sugar, apple butter, and pecans. Set aside.

In a large bowl, beat butter, cream cheese, and granulated sugar with a mixer at medium speed until creamy, 3 to 4 minutes, stopping to scrape sides of bowl. Add eggs, one at a time, beating well after each addition. Beat in vanilla.

In a medium bowl, whisk together flour, salt, cinnamon, and baking powder. Reduce mixer speed to low. Gradually add flour mixture to butter mixture, beating just until combined.

Spoon one-third of batter into prepared pan. Spoon half of apple butter mixture over batter in pan. Top with one-third of batter, remaining apple butter mixture, and remaining batter. Using a knife, pull blade back and forth through batter to swirl layers. Smooth top using an offset spatula.

Place pan in a cold oven. Bake at 300° until a wooden pick inserted near center comes out clean, about 1 hour and 20 minutes. Let cool in pan for 10 minutes. Remove from pan, and let cool completely on a wire rack. Drizzle with Glaze.

Glaze: In a medium saucepan, bring brown sugar, cream, butter, vanilla, and salt to a boil over medium-high heat. Cook, stirring constantly, until sugar is dissolved, about 3 minutes. Remove from heat, and let cool for 10 minutes. Whisk in confectioners' sugar.

Chocolate-Peanut Butter Pound Cake

MAKES ABOUT 10 SERVINGS

Cake

- ½ cup unsalted butter, softened
- ¾ cup creamy peanut butter
- 1 (8-ounce) package cream cheese, softened
- 3 cups sugar
- 1 tablespoon vanilla extract
- 6 large eggs
- 3½ cups all-purpose flour
- 1 teaspoon baking powder
- ½ teaspoon salt
- 1 cup plus 3 tablespoons heavy whipping cream, divided
- ¼ cup unsweetened cocoa powder
- 1 (4-ounce) bar bittersweet chocolate, melted

Chocolate Glaze
(recipe follows)
Garnish: chopped peanuts

Chocolate Glaze
Makes about 1 cup

- 2 (4-ounce) bars semisweet chocolate, chopped
- ¼ cup heavy whipping cream

Preheat oven to 325°. Spray a 12- to 15-cup Bundt pan with baking spray with flour.

Cake: In a large bowl, beat butter, peanut butter, cream cheese, sugar, and vanilla with a mixer at medium speed until creamy, 3 to 4 minutes, stopping to scrape sides of bowl. Add eggs, one at a time, beating well after each addition.

In a medium bowl, combine flour, baking powder, and salt. Reduce mixer speed to low. Gradually add flour mixture to butter mixture alternately with 1 cup cream, beginning and ending with flour mixture, beating just until combined after each addition. In a medium bowl, reserve 3 cups batter.

To reserved batter, add cocoa and remaining 3 tablespoons cream, stirring until smooth. Stir in melted chocolate. Alternately spoon peanut butter batter and chocolate batter into prepared pan. Gently swirl batters together with a knife.

Bake until a wooden pick inserted near center comes out clean, about 1 hour and 10 minutes. Let cool in pan for 10 minutes. Remove from pan, and let cool completely on a wire rack. Spoon Chocolate Glaze over cake. Garnish with chopped peanuts, if desired. Cover and refrigerate for up to 3 days.

Chocolate Glaze: In a small saucepan, combine chocolate and cream. Cook over low heat, stirring constantly, until chocolate is melted and mixture is smooth. Use immediately.

Peanut Butter Pound Cake

MAKES ABOUT 16 SERVINGS

1   cup unsalted butter,
      softened
1½   cups granulated sugar
1   cup firmly packed light
      brown sugar
½   cup creamy peanut butter
5   large eggs
1   teaspoon vanilla extract
3   cups all-purpose flour
½   teaspoon baking powder
¼   teaspoon salt
1   cup whole milk
1   (10-ounce) package
      swirled milk chocolate and
      peanut butter morsels
Garnish: confectioners' sugar,
      miniature chocolate-
      covered peanut butter
      cups

Preheat oven to 325°. Spray a 10- to 15-cup Bundt pan with baking spray with flour.

In a large bowl, beat butter, sugars, and peanut butter with a mixer at medium speed until fluffy, 3 to 4 minutes, stopping to scrape sides of bowl. Add eggs, one at a time, beating well after each addition. Beat in vanilla.

In a medium bowl, whisk together flour, baking powder, and salt. Reduce mixer speed to low. Gradually add flour mixture to butter mixture alternately with milk, beginning and ending with flour mixture, beating just until combined after each addition. Stir in swirled morsels. Spoon batter into prepared pan.

Bake until a wooden pick inserted near center comes out clean, 1 hour and 15 minutes to 1 hour and 25 minutes, covering with foil to prevent excess browning, if necessary. Let cool in pan for 10 minutes. Remove from pan, and let cool completely on a wire rack. Garnish with confectioners' sugar and peanut butter cups, if desired.

Peanut Butter and Honey Pound Cake

MAKES 8 TO 10 SERVINGS

1 cup unsalted butter, softened
½ cup creamy peanut butter
2 cups sugar
5 large eggs
½ cup half-and-half
1 teaspoon vanilla extract
2½ cups all-purpose flour
½ teaspoon salt
1 (10-ounce) bag peanut butter morsels
1 (8-ounce) package cream cheese, softened
¼ cup honey
2 tablespoons heavy whipping cream
Garnish: chopped dry-roasted peanuts, honey

Preheat oven to 300°. Spray a 10-cup Bundt pan with baking spray with flour.

In a large bowl, beat butter, peanut butter, and sugar with a mixer at medium speed until fluffy, 3 to 4 minutes, stopping to scrape sides of bowl. Add eggs, one at a time, beating well after each addition. Beat in half-and-half and vanilla.

In a medium bowl, whisk together flour and salt. Reduce mixer speed to low. Gradually add flour mixture to butter mixture, beating until combined. Stir in peanut butter morsels. Spoon batter into prepared pan.

Bake until a wooden pick inserted near center comes out clean, 1 hour and 10 minutes to 1 hour and 20 minutes, loosely covering with foil during last 20 minutes of baking to prevent excess browning. Let cool in pan for 10 minutes. Remove from pan, and let cool completely on a wire rack.

In a small bowl, beat cream cheese, honey, and cream with a mixer at medium speed until smooth. Drizzle over cooled cake. Garnish with peanuts and honey, if desired.

Candied Sweet Potato Bundt Cake

1   cup unsalted butter, softened
2   cups firmly packed dark brown sugar
1   (16-ounce) can candied yams (sweet potatoes), undrained
3   large eggs
3   cups all-purpose flour
2   tablespoons baking powder
1   teaspoon ground cinnamon
¼   teaspoon salt
½   cup whole buttermilk
1   teaspoon vanilla extract
1½   cups confectioners' sugar, sifted
¼   cup heavy whipping cream
Garnish: praline pecans

Preheat oven to 325°. Spray a 10- to 12-cup Bundt pan with baking spray with flour.

In a large bowl, beat butter and brown sugar with a mixer at medium speed until fluffy, 3 to 4 minutes, stopping to scrape sides of bowl. Beat in yams. Add eggs, one at a time, beating well after each addition.

In a medium bowl, whisk together flour, baking powder, cinnamon, and salt. Reduce mixer speed to low. Gradually add flour mixture to butter mixture alternately with buttermilk, beginning and ending with flour mixture, beating just until combined after each addition. Beat in vanilla. Spoon batter into prepared pan.

Bake until a wooden pick inserted near center comes out clean, 45 to 55 minutes. Let cool in pan 10 minutes. Remove from pan, and let cool completely on a wire rack.

In a small bowl, whisk together confectioners' sugar and cream until smooth. Spoon over cake. Garnish with praline pecans, if desired.

Brown Sugar Pound Cake

MAKES 12 TO 16 SERVINGS

Cake
1½ cups unsalted butter, softened
2 cups firmly packed light brown sugar
1 cup granulated sugar
5 large eggs
3 cups all-purpose flour
1 teaspoon baking powder
½ teaspoon salt
1 cup whole milk
1 (8-ounce) package toffee bits
1 cup chopped pecans
Caramel Drizzle (recipe follows)

Caramel Drizzle
Makes about 1½ cups
1 (14-ounce) can sweetened condensed milk
1 cup firmly packed light brown sugar
2 tablespoons unsalted butter
½ teaspoon vanilla extract

Preheat oven to 325°. Spray a 12-cup Bundt pan with baking spray with flour.

Cake: In a large bowl, beat butter and sugars with a mixer at medium speed until fluffy, 3 to 4 minutes, stopping to scrape sides of bowl. Add eggs, one at a time, beating well after each addition.

In a medium bowl, whisk together flour, baking powder, and salt. Reduce mixer speed to low. Gradually add flour mixture to butter mixture alternately with milk, beginning and ending with flour mixture, beating just until combined after each addition. Stir in toffee bits and pecans. Spoon batter into prepared pan.

Bake until a wooden pick inserted near center comes out clean, 1 hour and 15 minutes to 1 hour and 25 minutes, covering with foil to prevent excess browning, if necessary. Let cool in pan for 10 minutes. Remove from pan, and let cool completely on a wire rack. Spoon Caramel Drizzle over cooled cake.

Caramel Drizzle: In a medium saucepan, bring condensed milk and brown sugar to a boil over medium-high heat, whisking frequently. Reduce heat, and simmer for 8 minutes, whisking frequently. Remove from heat; whisk in butter and vanilla. Let cool for 5 minutes before using.

Pumpkin-Chocolate Swirl Bundt Cake

MAKES ABOUT 12 SERVINGS

1   cup plus 2 tablespoons unsalted butter, softened and divided

3¼   cups all-purpose flour, divided

1½   cups firmly packed dark brown sugar

3   large eggs

2   teaspoons baking powder

1   teaspoon baking soda

1   teaspoon salt

½   cup sour cream

1   teaspoon vanilla extract

1   cup canned pumpkin

1½   teaspoons pumpkin pie spice

⅓   cup half-and-half

2   tablespoons unsweetened cocoa powder

2   tablespoons confectioners' sugar

Preheat oven to 300°. Lightly coat a 10- to 15-cup Bundt pan with 2 tablespoons butter. Sprinkle with ¼ cup flour, rotating to coat bottom and sides of pan. Using a pastry brush, remove excess flour.

In a large bowl, beat brown sugar and remaining 1 cup butter with a mixer at medium speed until fluffy, 3 to 4 minutes, stopping to scrape sides of bowl. Add eggs, one at a time, beating well after each addition.

In a medium bowl, whisk together baking powder, baking soda, salt, and remaining 3 cups flour. Reduce mixer speed to low. Gradually add flour mixture to butter mixture, beating just until combined. Beat in sour cream and vanilla. Spoon 1 cup vanilla batter into a medium bowl.

Add pumpkin and pumpkin pie spice to remaining batter; beat until combined. Add half-and-half and cocoa to reserved 1 cup vanilla batter, whisking until combined. (Batters will be thick.)

Spoon one-third of pumpkin batter into prepared pan. Spoon half of chocolate batter by heaping teaspoonfuls over pumpkin batter. Repeat once, spooning remaining pumpkin batter on top. Gently swirl batters together with a knife, and smooth top with a spatula. Tap pan twice on counter to release any air bubbles.

Bake until a wooden pick inserted near center comes out clean, 55 to 60 minutes. Let cool in pan for 10 minutes. Remove from pan, and let cool completely on a wire rack. Dust with confectioners' sugar.

Pumpkin adds sweetness and tenderness to this marbled Bundt cake.

Easy Cinnamon Swirl Bundt Cake

Cake

1½ cups firmly packed light brown sugar, divided
Spice Blend (recipe follows)
1½ cups unsalted butter, softened
1½ cups granulated sugar
4   large eggs
2   teaspoons vanilla extract
4   cups all-purpose flour
2½ teaspoons baking powder
½   teaspoon salt
1½ cups sour cream
2   cups confectioners' sugar
3   tablespoons whole milk
2   tablespoons light corn syrup

Spice Blend
Makes about 2 tablespoons
2   teaspoons ground cinnamon
2   teaspoons ground cardamom
1   teaspoon ground cloves
1   teaspoon ground ginger
½   teaspoon ground white pepper

Preheat oven to 325°. Spray a 15-cup Bundt pan with baking spray with flour.

Cake: In a small bowl, stir together ½ cup brown sugar and Spice Blend. Set aside.

In the bowl of a stand mixer, beat butter, granulated sugar, and remaining 1 cup brown sugar at medium speed until fluffy, 3 to 4 minutes, stopping to scrape sides of bowl. Add eggs, one at a time, beating well after each addition. Beat in vanilla.

In a large bowl, whisk together flour, baking powder, and salt. Reduce speed of mixer to low. Gradually add flour mixture to butter mixture alternately with sour cream, beginning and ending with flour mixture, beating just until combined after each addition.

Pour one-third of batter into prepared pan. Sprinkle with half of sugared Spice Blend. Repeat procedure 1 time; top with remaining one-third of batter. Using a knife, swirl layers of batter and sugared Spice Blend together.

Bake until a wooden pick inserted near center comes out clean, about 1 hour and 20 minutes. Let cool in pan for 10 minutes. Remove from pan and let cool completely on a wire rack.

In a medium bowl, whisk together confectioners' sugar, milk, and corn syrup. Drizzle over cake.

Spice Blend: In a small bowl, stir together all ingredients until combined.

Gingerbread Bundt Cake

MAKES 10 TO 12 SERVINGS

Cake

1	cup unsalted butter, softened
1½	cups firmly packed dark brown sugar
½	cup granulated sugar
3	large eggs
3¾	cups all-purpose flour
2½	tablespoons ground ginger
2	teaspoons baking powder
2	teaspoons baking soda
1	teaspoon ground cinnamon
¾	teaspoon salt
¼	teaspoon ground cloves
1¾	cups whole buttermilk
½	cup dark unsulphured molasses
½	teaspoon lemon zest

Lemon Glaze (recipe follows)
Garnish: pomegranate seeds, fresh mint

Lemon Glaze
Makes about 1 cup

2	cups confectioners' sugar
2	tablespoons whole buttermilk
1	teaspoon lemon zest
¼	teaspoon fresh lemon juice

Preheat oven to 325°. Spray a 15-cup Bundt pan with baking spray with flour.

Cake: In large bowl, beat butter and sugars with a mixer at medium speed until fluffy, 3 to 4 minutes, stopping to scrape sides of bowl. Add eggs, one at a time, beating well after each addition.

In a large bowl, whisk together flour, ginger, baking powder, baking soda, cinnamon, salt, and cloves. In a small bowl, stir together buttermilk, molasses, and zest.

Reduce mixer speed to low. Gradually add flour mixture to butter mixture alternately with buttermilk mixture, beginning and ending with flour mixture, beating just until combined after each addition. Pour batter into prepared pan.

Bake until a wooden pick inserted near center comes out clean, 45 to 50 minutes. Let cool in pan for 10 minutes. Remove from pan, and let cool completely on a wire rack. Drizzle with Lemon Glaze. Garnish with pomegranate seeds and mint, if desired.

Lemon Glaze: In a medium bowl, whisk together all ingredients until smooth.

Ginger Pound Cake with Maple Glaze

Cake
- ½ cup unsalted butter, softened
- ½ cup all-vegetable shortening
- 2 cups granulated sugar
- 5 large eggs
- 1½ teaspoons vanilla extract
- 2 cups all-purpose flour
- 1 tablespoon ground ginger
- ¼ teaspoon salt
- ½ cup whole milk
- Garnish: chopped candied ginger, chopped pecans

Maple Glaze
- ½ cup confectioners' sugar
- 3 to 4 tablespoons maple syrup
- 1 teaspoon maple flavoring

Preheat oven to 300°. Spray a 10- to 15-cup Bundt pan with baking spray with flour.

Cake: In large bowl, beat butter, shortening, and granulated sugar with a mixer at medium speed until fluffy, 3 to 4 minutes, stopping to scrape sides of bowl. Add eggs, one at a time, beating well after each addition. Beat in vanilla.

In medium bowl, sift together flour, ginger, and salt. Reduce mixer speed to low. Gradually add flour mixture to butter mixture alternately with milk, beginning and ending with flour mixture, beating just until combined after each addition. Spoon batter into prepared pan.

Bake until a wooden pick inserted near center comes out clean, 1 hour and 10 minutes to 1 hour and 15 minutes, loosely covering with foil during last 20 minutes of baking to prevent excess browning. Let cool in pan for 10 minutes. Remove from pan, and let cool completely on a wire rack. Drizzle Maple Glaze over cake. Garnish with candied ginger and pecans, if desired.

Maple Glaze: In small bowl, combine confectioners' sugar, 3 tablespoons maple syrup, and maple flavoring. Add remaining 1 tablespoon maple syrup if a thinner consistency is desired.

German Chocolate Pound Cake

Cake
1	cup unsalted butter, softened
2	cups sugar
4	large eggs
1	cup sour cream
1	teaspoon vanilla extract
2	cups all-purpose flour
2	tablespoons natural unsweetened cocoa powder
½	teaspoon baking soda
½	teaspoon salt
1	(4-ounce) bar German's sweet chocolate, melted and cooled

Coconut-Pecan Frosting (recipe follows)

Coconut-Pecan Frosting
Makes about 2 cups
1	(5-ounce) can evaporated milk
¾	cup sugar
⅓	cup butter
2	egg yolks
1½	cups sweetened flaked coconut
¾	cup chopped pecans

Preheat oven to 325°. Spray a 10- to 15-cup Bundt pan with baking spray with flour.

Cake: In a large bowl, beat butter and sugar with a mixer at medium speed until fluffy, 3 to 4 minutes, stopping to scrape sides of bowl. Add eggs, one at a time, beating well after each addition. Beat in sour cream and vanilla.

In a medium bowl, whisk together flour, cocoa, baking soda, and salt. Reduce mixer speed to low. Gradually add flour mixture to butter mixture, beating just until combined. Add chocolate, beating until combined. Spoon batter into prepared pan.

Bake until a wooden pick inserted near center comes out clean, about 1 hour. Let cool in pan for 10 minutes. Remove from pan, and let cool completely on a wire rack. Spoon Coconut-Pecan Frosting on top of cooled cake.

Coconut-Pecan Frosting: In a medium saucepan, combine evaporated milk, sugar, butter, and egg yolks. Cook over medium heat, stirring constantly, until thickened and golden brown, about 15 minutes. Remove from heat; stir in coconut and pecans.

Chocolate-Coconut Bundt Cake

MAKES 10 TO 12 SERVINGS

Cake

1	cup unsalted butter
1½	cups granulated sugar
3	large eggs
2	cups all-purpose flour
¼	cup unsweetened cocoa powder
1	teaspoon baking soda
¾	teaspoon salt
½	teaspoon baking powder
1	cup water
1	teaspoon vanilla extract

Filling

1	cup sweetened flaked coconut
2	tablespoons granulated sugar
2	tablespoons all-purpose flour
½	teaspoon vanilla extract
⅛	teaspoon salt
1	large egg white
½	cup dark chocolate morsels

Glaze

1½	cups confectioners' sugar
3 to 4	tablespoons coconut milk

Preheat oven to 350°. Spray a 15-cup Bundt pan with baking spray with flour.

Cake: In a large bowl, beat butter and sugar with a mixer at medium speed until fluffy, 3 to 4 minutes, stopping to scrape sides of bowl. Add eggs, one at a time, beating well after each addition.

In a medium bowl, whisk together flour, cocoa, baking soda, salt, and baking powder. Reduce mixer speed to low. Gradually add flour mixture to butter mixture alternately with 1 cup water, beginning and ending with flour mixture, beating just until combined after each addition. Beat in vanilla.

Filling: In a medium bowl, combine coconut, sugar, flour, vanilla, salt, and egg white. Stir in chocolate.

Spoon half of batter into prepared pan. Spoon coconut mixture over batter, avoiding edges of pan. Spoon remaining batter over coconut mixture. Smooth top with an offset spatula.

Bake until a wooden pick inserted near center comes out clean, about 45 minutes. Let cool in pan for 15 minutes. Remove from pan, and let cool completely on a wire rack.

Glaze: In a medium bowl, place confectioners' sugar. Whisk in coconut milk, 1 tablespoon at a time, until glaze reaches a thick consistency. Spoon glaze over cake. Let stand until glaze is set, about 30 minutes.

Double Chocolate-Spice Bundt Cake

2 tablespoons unsalted butter, softened
¼ cup all-purpose flour

Cake
1 cup whole milk
2 chai tea bags
1 cup unsalted butter, softened
1½ cups firmly packed dark brown sugar
3 large eggs
3 cups all-purpose flour
¾ teaspoon baking powder
½ teaspoon baking soda
½ teaspoon salt
1 cup whole buttermilk
2 (4-ounce) bars bittersweet chocolate, finely chopped
1 cup semisweet chocolate morsels, melted and slightly cooled
1 teaspoon vanilla extract

Glaze
3 ounces bittersweet chocolate, melted
1½ cups confectioners' sugar
1 tablespoon unsalted butter

Preheat oven to 300°. Lightly coat a 10- to 15-cup Bundt pan with butter. Sprinkle with flour, rotating to coat bottom and sides of pan. Using a pastry brush, remove excess flour.

Cake: In a small saucepan, bring milk to a simmer over medium heat. Remove from heat. Add tea bags; cover and let stand for 10 minutes. Discard tea bags. Reserve ½ cup chai milk for batter and 5 tablespoons chai milk for glaze.

In a large bowl, beat butter and brown sugar with a mixer at medium speed until fluffy, 3 to 4 minutes, stopping to scrape sides of bowl. Add eggs, one at a time, beating well after each addition.

In a medium bowl, whisk together flour, baking powder, baking soda, and salt. In a small bowl, whisk together buttermilk and reserved ½ cup chai milk.

Reduce mixer speed to low. Gradually add flour mixture to butter mixture alternately with buttermilk mixture, beginning and ending with flour mixture, beating just until combined after each addition. Add chopped chocolate, melted chocolate, and vanilla, beating just until combined. Spoon batter into prepared pan, smoothing top using an offset spatula. Tap pan twice on counter to release any air bubbles.

Bake until a wooden pick inserted near center comes out clean, about 1 hour and 10 minutes. Let cool in pan for 10 minutes. Remove from pan, and let cool completely on a wire rack.

Glaze: In a medium bowl, whisk together melted chocolate, confectioners' sugar, butter, and enough remaining chai milk, 1 tablespoon at a time, until a smooth consistency is reached. Drizzle over cake.

Rich chocolate and chai spices make this cake perfect for any chocolate lover.

Chocolate Pound Cake with Tasty Hot Fudge Sauce

MAKES ABOUT 10 SERVINGS

Cake
1½ cups unsalted butter, softened
3 cups granulated sugar
5 large eggs
1 teaspoon vanilla extract
3 cups all-purpose flour
5 tablespoons special dark cocoa powder*
½ teaspoon baking soda
½ teaspoon baking powder
½ teaspoon salt
¾ cup whole buttermilk
½ cup sour cream
Tasty Hot Fudge Sauce (recipe follows)
Garnish: confectioners' sugar

Tasty Hot Fudge Sauce
Makes about 2½ cups
¾ (4-ounce) bar unsweetened chocolate, chopped
½ cup unsalted butter
1 cup granulated sugar
½ cup firmly packed brown sugar
1 cup heavy whipping cream
1 teaspoon vanilla extract

Preheat oven to 325°. Spray a 12- to 15-cup Bundt pan with baking spray with flour.

Cake: In a large bowl, beat butter and sugar with a mixer at medium speed until fluffy, 3 to 4 minutes, stopping to scrape sides of bowl. Add eggs, one at a time, beating well after each addition. Beat in vanilla.

In a medium bowl, whisk together flour, cocoa, baking soda, baking powder, and salt. Reduce mixer speed to low. Gradually add flour mixture to butter mixture alternately with buttermilk, beginning and ending with flour mixture, beating just until combined after each addition. Stir in sour cream. Pour batter into prepared pan.

Bake until a wooden pick inserted near center comes out clean, about 1 hour. Let cool in pan for 10 minutes. Remove from pan, and let cool completely on a wire rack. Serve with Tasty Hot Fudge Sauce. Garnish with confectioners' sugar, if desired.

Tasty Hot Fudge Sauce: In a medium saucepan, heat chocolate and butter over medium heat. Cook, stirring frequently, until chocolate is melted and mixture is smooth. Stir in sugars. Add cream; bring to a boil over medium-high heat. Reduce heat, and simmer for 5 minutes, stirring frequently. Remove from heat, and stir in vanilla. Cover and refrigerate for up to 1 week.

*We used Hershey's Special Dark Cocoa Powder.

Chocolate Bundt Cake with Baileys Custard Glaze

MAKES 8 TO 10 SERVINGS

Cake

1	cup unsalted butter, softened
1½	cups sugar
4	large eggs
1	teaspoon vanilla extract
2½	cups all-purpose flour
½	cup unsweetened cocoa powder
1	teaspoon baking soda
¾	teaspoon salt
1	cup whole buttermilk

Baileys Custard Glaze (recipe follows)
Garnish: grated chocolate

Baileys Custard Glaze
Makes about 1 cup

1	cup Irish cream liqueur*
2	large eggs
¼	cup sugar
2	tablespoons unsalted butter
1	teaspoon vanilla extract

Preheat oven to 325°. Spray a 15-cup Bundt pan with baking spray with flour.

Cake: In a large bowl, beat butter and sugar with a mixer at medium speed until fluffy, 3 to 4 minutes, stopping to scrape sides of bowl. Add eggs, one at a time, beating well after each addition. Beat in vanilla.

In a medium bowl, whisk together flour, cocoa, baking soda, and salt. Reduce mixer speed to low. Gradually add flour mixture to butter mixture alternately with buttermilk, beginning and ending with flour mixture, beating just until combined after each addition. Spoon batter into prepared pan.

Bake until a wooden pick inserted near center comes out clean, about 1 hour. Let cool completely in pan. Invert onto a serving platter. Drizzle with Baileys Custard Glaze. Garnish with grated chocolate, if desired.

Baileys Custard Glaze: In a small saucepan, heat liqueur over medium heat until simmering.

In a medium bowl, whisk together eggs and sugar. Add hot liqueur, ½ cup at a time, whisking rapidly and constantly until well combined. Return mixture to saucepan; cook, stirring constantly, until thickened, about 1 minute. Pour into a clean bowl; whisk in butter and vanilla. Let cool. Refrigerate until ready to use.

*We used Baileys Original Irish Cream.

Chocolate Bundt Cake

1½   cups unsalted butter,
      softened
2½   cups sugar
4   large eggs
2   teaspoons vanilla extract
2¾   cups all-purpose flour
½   cup unsweetened cocoa
      powder
1½   teaspoons salt
1   teaspoon baking powder
1   teaspoon baking soda
1   cup hot coffee
2   (4-ounce) bars bittersweet
      chocolate, chopped
1   cup whole buttermilk
1   (12.25-ounce) jar caramel
      sauce,* unheated
⅓   cup chopped toasted
      pecans

Preheat oven to 325°. Spray a 15-cup Bundt pan with baking spray with flour.

In a large bowl, beat butter and sugar with a mixer at medium speed until fluffy, 3 to 4 minutes, stopping to scrape sides of bowl. Add eggs, one at a time, beating well after each addition. Beat in vanilla.

In a medium bowl, whisk together flour, cocoa, salt, baking powder, and baking soda. In a small bowl, stir together coffee and chocolate until melted; stir in buttermilk.

Reduce mixer speed to low. Gradually add flour mixture to butter mixture alternately with chocolate mixture, beginning and ending with flour mixture, beating just until combined after each addition. Spoon batter into prepared pan.

Bake until a wooden pick inserted near center comes out clean, about 1 hour and 5 minutes. Let cool in pan for 10 minutes. Remove from pan, and let cool completely on a wire rack. Drizzle with caramel sauce, and top with pecans.

*We used Smucker's Hot Caramel Topping.

German Chocolate Bundt Cake with Butterscotch Glaze

MAKES 8 TO 10 SERVINGS

Cake
¾ cup unsweetened cocoa powder
¾ (4-ounce) bar German's sweet chocolate, chopped
¾ cup hot coffee
½ cup unsalted butter, softened
2 cups sugar
3 teaspoons vanilla extract
3 egg whites, room temperature
3 cups all-purpose flour
3 teaspoons baking powder
1½ teaspoons salt
¾ teaspoon baking soda
1½ cups whole buttermilk
Butterscotch Glaze (recipe follows)

Butterscotch Glaze
Makes about 1 cup
1 cup butterscotch morsels
½ cup half-and-half

Preheat oven to 350°. Spray a 10-cup Bundt pan with baking spray with flour.

Cake: In a medium bowl, whisk together cocoa, chocolate, and coffee. Set aside.

In a large bowl, beat butter, sugar, and vanilla with a mixer at medium speed until fluffy, 3 to 4 minutes, stopping to scrape sides of bowl. Add egg whites, one at a time, beating well after each addition. Reduce mixer speed to low, and add chocolate mixture, beating until combined.

In another medium bowl, whisk together flour, baking powder, salt, and baking soda. Gradually add flour mixture to butter mixture alternately with buttermilk, beginning and ending with flour mixture, beating just until combined after each addition. Pour batter into prepared pan.

Bake until a wooden pick inserted near center comes out clean, about 1 hour. Let cool in pan for 10 minutes. Remove from pan, and let cool completely on a wire rack. Pour Butterscotch Glaze over cake. Store at room temperature for up to 5 days.

Butterscotch Glaze: In a small saucepan, combine butterscotch morsels and half-and-half. Cook over medium heat, whisking frequently, until mixture is smooth and morsels are melted. Let cool until thickened, about 15 minutes. Use immediately. If glaze becomes firm, place in a microwavable bowl, and microwave on high until melted and smooth, 10 to 15 seconds.

Chocolate Pound Cake

Cake
- 1 (4-ounce) bar semisweet chocolate, chopped
- 1 (4-ounce) bar bittersweet chocolate, chopped
- 1 cup unsalted butter, softened
- 1½ cups granulated sugar
- 4 large eggs
- ½ cup dark corn syrup
- 1 tablespoon vanilla extract
- 2¼ cups all-purpose flour
- ¼ cup unsweetened cocoa powder
- ½ teaspoon salt
- ¼ teaspoon baking soda
- 1 cup whole buttermilk
- Buttermilk Glaze (recipe follows)
- Garnish: sugared cranberries, sugared rosemary

Buttermilk Glaze
Makes 2 cups
- 2 cups confectioners' sugar
- ½ cup whole buttermilk
- 1 teaspoon vanilla extract

Preheat oven to 325°. Spray a 15-cup Bundt pan with baking spray with flour.

Cake: In a medium microwave-safe bowl, heat chocolates on high in 30-second intervals, stirring between each, until melted and smooth (about 1½ minutes total).

In a large bowl, beat butter and sugar with a mixer at medium speed until fluffy, 3 to 4 minutes, stopping to scrape sides of bowl. Add eggs, one at a time, beating well after each addition. Add corn syrup, vanilla, and melted chocolate, beating to combine.

In a medium bowl, whisk together flour, cocoa, salt, and baking soda. Reduce mixer speed to low. Gradually add flour mixture to butter mixture alternately with buttermilk, beginning and ending with flour mixture, beating just until combined after each addition. Pour batter into prepared pan.

Bake until a wooden pick inserted near center comes out clean, about 1 hour and 10 minutes. Let cool in pan for 10 minutes. Remove from pan, and let cool completely on a wire rack. Pour Buttermilk Glaze over cooled cake. Garnish with sugared cranberries and sugared rosemary, if desired.

Buttermilk Glaze: In a small bowl, whisk together confectioners' sugar and buttermilk until smooth. Add vanilla, and stir to combine. Use immediately.

Cream Cheese-Filled Red Velvet Pound Cake

MAKES ABOUT 10 SERVINGS

Cake

1½	cups unsalted butter, softened
3	cups granulated sugar
5	large eggs
1	teaspoon distilled white vinegar
1	teaspoon vanilla extract
3	cups all-purpose flour
⅓	cup unsweetened cocoa powder
½	teaspoon salt
¼	teaspoon baking soda
1	cup whole buttermilk
1	(1-ounce) bottle liquid red food coloring
	Cream Cheese Filling (recipe follows)
1	cup confectioners' sugar
2	tablespoons heavy whipping cream

Cream Cheese Filling
Makes about 1 cup

1	(8-ounce) package cream cheese, softened
⅓	cup granulated sugar
1	large egg
1	teaspoon vanilla extract

Preheat oven to 325°. Spray a 12- to 15-cup Bundt pan with baking spray with flour.

Cake: In a large bowl, beat butter and granulated sugar with a mixer at medium speed until fluffy, 3 to 4 minutes, stopping to scrape sides of bowl. Add eggs, one at a time, beating well after each addition. Beat in vinegar and vanilla.

In a medium bowl, combine flour, cocoa, salt, and baking soda. Reduce mixer speed to low. Gradually add flour mixture to butter mixture alternately with buttermilk, beginning and ending with flour mixture, beating just until combined after each addition. Stir in food coloring. Spoon half of batter into prepared pan. Top with Cream Cheese Filling. Spoon remaining batter over filling.

Bake until a wooden pick inserted near center comes out clean, 1 hour and 10 minutes to 1 hour and 15 minutes. Let cool in pan for 10 minutes. Remove from pan, and let cool completely on a wire rack.

In a small bowl, whisk together confectioners' sugar and cream until smooth. Drizzle over cooled cake, and sprinkle with cake crumbles, if desired. Cover and refrigerate for up to 3 days.

Cream Cheese Filling: In a small bowl, beat cream cheese and sugar with a mixer at medium speed until smooth. Add egg and vanilla, beating until combined.

Red Velvet Pound Cake

Cake

1½	cups unsalted butter, softened
3	cups granulated sugar
5	large eggs
3	cups all-purpose flour
⅓	cup unsweetened cocoa powder
½	teaspoon salt
¼	teaspoon baking soda
1	cup whole buttermilk
1	(1-ounce) bottle liquid red food coloring
1	teaspoon distilled white vinegar
1	teaspoon vanilla extract

Cream Cheese Glaze (recipe follows)

Cream Cheese Glaze
Makes about ¾ cup

1	(3-ounce) package cream cheese, softened
1½	cups confectioners' sugar
1	tablespoon milk

Preheat oven to 350°. Spray a 12-cup Bundt pan with baking spray with flour.

Cake: In a large bowl, beat butter and sugar with a mixer at medium speed until fluffy, 3 to 4 minutes, stopping to scrape sides of bowl. Add eggs, one at a time, beating well after each addition.

In a medium bowl, combine flour, cocoa, salt, and baking soda. In a small bowl, combine buttermilk, food coloring, vinegar, and vanilla. Reduce mixer speed to low. Gradually add flour mixture to butter mixture alternately with buttermilk mixture, beating just until combined after each addition. Spoon batter into prepared pan.

Bake until a wooden pick inserted near center comes out clean, 50 to 60 minutes. Let cool in pan for 10 minutes. Remove from pan, and let cool completely on a wire rack. Drizzle cooled cake with Cream Cheese Glaze.

Cream Cheese Glaze: In a small bowl, beat cream cheese with a mixer at low speed until creamy. Gradually add confectioners' sugar, beating until combined. Add milk, beating until smooth.

Vanilla Pound Cake with Peppermint Glaze

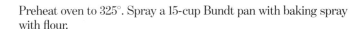

MAKES 10 TO 12 SERVINGS

Cake
1   cup unsalted butter,
     softened
½   cup butter-flavored
     shortening
3   cups granulated sugar
5   large eggs
½   vanilla bean, split
     lengthwise, seeds scraped
     and reserved
3   cups all-purpose flour
1   tablespoon vanilla
     powder*
1   teaspoon salt
½   teaspoon baking powder
1   cup whole buttermilk
2   teaspoons vanilla extract
Peppermint Glaze
     (recipe follows)
Garnish: crushed peppermints

Peppermint Glaze
Makes about 1½ cups
1½   cups confectioners' sugar
3   tablespoons whole milk
½   teaspoon peppermint
     extract

Preheat oven to 325°. Spray a 15-cup Bundt pan with baking spray with flour.

Cake: In a large bowl, beat butter, shortening, and sugar with a mixer at medium speed until fluffy, 3 to 4 minutes, stopping to scrape sides of bowl. Add eggs, one at a time, beating well after each addition. Beat in vanilla bean seeds.

In a medium bowl, sift together flour, vanilla powder, salt, and baking powder. In a small bowl, stir together buttermilk and vanilla extract. Reduce mixer speed to low. Gradually add flour mixture to butter mixture alternately with buttermilk mixture, beginning and ending with flour mixture, beating just until combined after each addition. Pour batter into prepared pan. Tap pan on counter to release any air bubbles.

Bake for 45 minutes. Cover with foil, and bake until a wooden pick inserted near center comes out clean, about 45 minutes more. Let cool in pan for 20 minutes. Remove from pan, and let cool completely on a wire rack. Pour Peppermint Glaze over cooled cake. Garnish with crushed peppermints, if desired. Cover and refrigerate for up to 5 days.

Peppermint Glaze: In a small bowl, whisk together confectioners' sugar, milk, and peppermint extract until smooth. Use immediately.

*We used Nielsen-Massey Madagascar Bourbon Pure Vanilla Powder, which can be purchased at specialty foods stores or online.

Candied Apple-Pear Bundt Cake

MAKES 10 TO 12 SERVINGS

Cake

3	cups granulated sugar, divided
½	cup cane syrup*
1½	cups plus 2 tablespoons unsalted butter, softened and divided
2	large Granny Smith apples, peeled, cored, and sliced
2	Bosc pears, peeled, cored, and sliced
5	large eggs
3	cups all-purpose flour
2	teaspoons ground cinnamon
1	teaspoon grated fresh nutmeg
1	teaspoon salt
½	teaspoon baking soda
1	cup sour cream
2	teaspoons vanilla extract
	Cane Syrup Glaze (recipe follows)

Cane Syrup Glaze
Makes about 1 cup

2	cups confectioners' sugar
2	tablespoons whole buttermilk

Preheat oven to 325°. Spray a 15-cup Bundt pan with baking spray with flour.

Cake: In a large skillet, bring 1 cup sugar and cane syrup to a boil over medium-high heat. Cook, stirring constantly, until sugar dissolves, about 2 minutes. Stir in 2 tablespoons butter until melted. Add apple and pear, stirring to combine. Reduce heat to medium; cook, stirring occasionally, until fruit softens, about 12 minutes. Remove from heat, and let cool completely.

In a large bowl, beat remaining 1½ cups butter and remaining 2 cups sugar with a mixer at medium speed until fluffy, 3 to 4 minutes, stopping to scrape sides of bowl. Add eggs, one at a time, beating well after each addition.

In a medium bowl, stir together flour, cinnamon, nutmeg, salt, and baking soda. Reduce mixer speed to low. Gradually add flour mixture to butter mixture alternately with sour cream, beginning and ending with flour mixture, beating just until combined after each addition. Beat in vanilla.

Reserve ⅔ cup syrup from fruit mixture for Cane Syrup Glaze. Gently fold remaining syrup and fruit mixture into batter. Spoon batter into prepared pan.

Bake until a wooden pick inserted near center comes out clean, about 1 hour and 10 minutes. Let cool in pan for 10 minutes. Remove from pan, and let cool completely on a wire rack. Drizzle with Cane Syrup Glaze.

Cane Syrup Glaze: In a small bowl, stir together reserved ⅔ cup syrup, confectioners' sugar, and buttermilk until smooth.

*We used Steen's Pure Cane Syrup.

Kentucky Browned Butter Bundt Cake

MAKES 8 TO 10 SERVINGS

1 cup plus 2 tablespoons unsalted butter, softened and divided
2 cups plus 6 tablespoons sugar, divided
4 large eggs
3 cups all-purpose flour
1½ teaspoons salt
1 teaspoon baking powder
½ teaspoon baking soda
½ teaspoon ground nutmeg
½ teaspoon ground cloves
¼ teaspoon ground cardamom
1 cup whole buttermilk
4 teaspoons vanilla extract, divided
1 tablespoon water
Fresh cranberries, to serve

Preheat oven to 325°. Spray a 10-cup Bundt pan with baking spray with flour.

In a large bowl, beat 1 cup butter and 2 cups sugar with a mixer at medium speed until fluffy, 3 to 4 minutes, stopping to scrape sides of bowl. Add eggs, one at a time, beating just until combined after each addition.

In another large bowl, whisk together flour, salt, baking powder, baking soda, nutmeg, cloves, and cardamom. In a small bowl, stir together buttermilk and 3 teaspoons vanilla.

Reduce mixer speed to low. Gradually add flour mixture to butter mixture alternately with buttermilk mixture, beginning and ending with flour mixture, beating just until combined after each addition. Pour batter into prepared pan.

Bake until a wooden pick inserted near center comes out clean, 60 to 65 minutes. Let cool in pan for 15 minutes; invert onto a serving plate.

In a small saucepan, melt remaining 2 tablespoons butter over medium-low heat. Cook until butter is light brown, about 12 minutes. Add 1 tablespoon water, remaining 6 tablespoons sugar, and remaining 1 teaspoon vanilla; bring to a simmer. Cook, stirring frequently, until sugar is dissolved, about 1 minute. Pour glaze over warm cake. Let cool completely until sugar has crystalized, about 1 hour. Serve with cranberries, if desired.

loaves & mini cakes

Versatile loaf and mini loaf pans, as well as
baking cups, are useful for pound cake loaves and mini
cakes. Individual servings can be created in a snap!

Buttermilk Pound Cake

Cake
¾ cup unsalted butter, softened
1½ cups granulated sugar
3 large eggs, room temperature
1½ cups all-purpose flour, sifted
½ teaspoon salt
½ cup whole buttermilk
Buttermilk Whipped Cream (recipe follows)

Buttermilk Whipped Cream
Makes about 4 cups
1½ cups heavy whipping cream
¾ cup whole buttermilk
½ cup confectioners' sugar

Spray a 9x5-inch loaf pan with baking spray with flour. Line pan with parchment paper, and spray pan again.

Cake: In a large bowl, beat butter and sugar with a mixer at medium speed until fluffy, 3 to 4 minutes, stopping to scrape sides of bowl. Add eggs, one at a time, beating well after each addition.

In a medium bowl, whisk together flour and salt. Reduce mixer speed to low. Gradually add flour mixture to butter mixture alternately with buttermilk, beginning and ending with flour mixture, beating just until combined after each addition. Spoon batter into prepared pan.

Place pan in a cold oven. Bake at 300° until a wooden pick inserted in center comes out clean, about 1 hour and 20 minutes. Let cool in pan for 10 minutes. Remove from pan, and let cool completely on a wire rack. Serve with Buttermilk Whipped Cream.

Buttermilk Whipped Cream: In a large bowl, beat cream, buttermilk, and confectioners' sugar with a mixer at high speed until soft peaks form, about 2 minutes. Serve immediately.

Browned Butter-Cinnamon Marble Pound Cake with Buttermilk Glaze

MAKES 2 (9X5-INCH) LOAVES

Cake
1	cup Browned Butter (recipe follows), room temperature
2¼	cups granulated sugar, divided
4	large eggs
3	cups all-purpose flour
1	tablespoon baking powder
3	tablespoons ground cinnamon, divided
1½	teaspoons salt, divided
1¼	cup whole buttermilk
2	tablespoons vanilla extract

Buttermilk Glaze
   (recipe follows)
Garnish: chopped pecans

Browned Butter
Makes 1 cup
1¼   cups unsalted butter

Buttermilk Glaze
Makes 1½ cups
1½   cups confectioners' sugar
¼   cup whole buttermilk
½   teaspoon vanilla extract

Preheat oven to 350°. Spray 2 (9x5-inch) loaf pans with baking spray. Line bottom of pans with parchment paper, and spray pans again.

Cake: In a large bowl, beat Browned Butter and 2 cups sugar with a mixer at medium speed until fluffy, 3 to 4 minutes, stopping to scrape sides of bowl. Add eggs, one at a time, beating well after each addition.

In a medium bowl, whisk together flour, baking powder, 1 tablespoon cinnamon, and 1 teaspoon salt. In a small bowl, whisk together buttermilk and vanilla. Reduce mixer speed to low. Gradually add flour mixture to butter mixture alternately with buttermilk mixture, beginning and ending with flour mixture, beating just until combined after each addition.

In a small bowl, whisk together remaining ¼ cup sugar, remaining 2 tablespoons cinnamon, and remaining ½ teaspoon salt.

Spoon a thin layer of batter into prepared pans. Sprinkle with 2 tablespoons cinnamon mixture, covering entire surface of batter. Repeat process twice, ending with batter. Pull a wooden skewer through batter in a swirling pattern. Tap pans on counter to release any air bubbles.

Bake until a wooden pick inserted in center comes out clean, 55 minutes to 1 hour and 10 minutes. Let cool in pans for 10 minutes. Remove from pans, and let cool completely on a wire rack. Spoon Buttermilk Glaze over cakes. Garnish with pecans, if desired. Cover and refrigerate for up to 5 days.

Browned Butter: In a medium saucepan, cook butter over medium heat, stirring occasionally, until butter turns a medium-brown color and has a nutty aroma. Remove from heat, and strain through a fine-mesh sieve. Cover and refrigerate for up to 3 days. Bring to room temperature before using.

Buttermilk Glaze: In a small bowl, whisk together all ingredients until smooth. Use immediately.

Banana Pound Cake with Peanut Butter Swirl

Cake

1	cup unsalted butter, softened
1½	cups sugar
6	large eggs
3	cups all-purpose flour
1½	teaspoons baking powder
1	teaspoon baking soda
1	teaspoon salt
1½	cups mashed banana (about 3 large bananas)
½	cup sour cream
1	tablespoon vanilla extract

Peanut Butter Swirl

½	(8-ounce) package cream cheese, softened
¼	cup creamy peanut butter
¼	cup sugar
¼	cup unsweetened cocoa powder
1	large egg
1	tablespoon all-purpose flour

Glaze

½	cup heavy whipping cream
1	cup semisweet chocolate morsels

Preheat oven to 325°. Spray 2 (9x5-inch) loaf pans with baking spray with flour.

Cake: In a large bowl, beat butter and sugar with a mixer at medium speed until fluffy, 3 to 4 minutes, stopping to scrape sides of bowl. Add eggs, one at a time, beating well after each addition.

In a medium bowl, whisk together flour, baking powder, baking soda, and salt. Reduce mixer speed to low. Gradually add flour mixture to butter mixture, beating just until combined after each addition. Stir in mashed banana, sour cream, and vanilla.

Peanut Butter Swirl: In a medium bowl, beat cream cheese, peanut butter, sugar, cocoa, egg, and flour with a mixer at medium speed until smooth.

Divide one-third of batter between prepared pans. Spoon half of swirl mixture over batter in each pan, avoiding edges of pan. Repeat layers with remaining banana batter and swirl batter. Using a knife, pull blade back and forth through batter to swirl. Smooth tops using an offset spatula.

Bake until a wooden pick inserted in center comes out clean, about 1 hour. Let cool in pans for 15 minutes. Remove from pans, and let cool completely on wire racks.

Glaze: In a microwave-safe bowl, microwave cream for 1 minute. Add chocolate morsels, stirring until smooth. Drizzle Glaze over cooled cake. Serve immediately.

Sweet Tea Poke Pound Cake with Lemon Glaze

MAKES 2 (8X4-INCH) LOAVES

1⅔ cups whole milk

8 family-size tea bags, divided

2 cups plus 2 tablespoons unsalted butter, softened and divided

4½ cups granulated sugar, divided

4 large eggs

2 teaspoons vanilla extract

4 cups all-purpose flour

1½ teaspoons salt

1 teaspoon baking powder

1 cup water

1 tablespoon lemon zest

¼ cup fresh lemon juice

2 tablespoons heavy whipping cream

1 tablespoon light corn syrup

1¾ cups confectioners' sugar

Garnish: lemon slices

cake tip
After pouring syrup over loaves, you can freeze them for later use.

Preheat oven to 325°. Spray 2 (8x4-inch) loaf pans with baking spray with flour.

In a small saucepan, bring milk and 4 tea bags to a simmer over medium heat, stirring frequently. Remove from heat, and let steep for 5 minutes. Press tea bags to release excess liquid; discard tea bags. Measure 1⅓ cups milk mixture. Refrigerate to let cool completely.

In a large bowl, beat 2 cups butter and 3 cups granulated sugar with a mixer at medium speed until fluffy, 3 to 4 minutes, stopping to scrape sides of bowl. Add eggs, one at a time, beating well after each addition. Beat in vanilla.

In another large bowl, whisk together together flour, salt, and baking powder. Reduce mixer speed to low. Gradually add flour mixture to butter mixture alternately with milk mixture, beginning and ending with flour mixture, beating just until combined after each addition. Divide batter between prepared pans.

Bake until a wooden pick inserted in center comes out clean, about 1 hour and 35 minutes. Let cool in pans for 20 minutes.

In a small saucepan, bring 1 cup water, 1 cup granulated sugar, and remaining 4 tea bags to a boil over medium-high heat. Remove from heat, and let steep for 5 minutes. Press tea bags to release excess liquid; discard tea bags. Let syrup cool at room temperature.

Using a wooden pick, poke holes in warm loaves. Carefully pour syrup over loaves. Let cool completely.

In a small saucepan, bring lemon zest and juice, cream, corn syrup, remaining ½ cup granulated sugar, and remaining 2 tablespoons butter to a boil over medium-high heat. Reduce heat to medium-low; cook for 1 minute. Remove from heat; add confectioners' sugar, and whisk for 1 minute. Let cool for 3 minutes. Pour glaze over cooled loaves. Garnish with lemon slices, if desired.

Mini Pound Cakes

MAKES 7 (6X3-INCH) LOAVES

1   cup unsalted butter,
     softened
3   cups sugar
5   large eggs
1   cup low-fat vanilla yogurt
¼   cup heavy whipping cream
½   teaspoon vanilla extract
3½   cups cake flour*
¼   teaspoon salt
¼   teaspoon baking soda
Jam, to serve

Preheat oven to 300°. Spray 7 (6x3-inch) miniature loaf pans with baking spray with flour.

In a large bowl, beat butter and sugar with a mixer at medium speed until fluffy, 3 to 4 minutes, stopping to scrape sides of bowl. Add eggs, one at a time, beating well after each addition. Beat in yogurt, cream, and vanilla.

In a medium bowl, whisk together flour, salt, and baking soda. Reduce mixer speed to low. Gradually add flour mixture to butter mixture, beating until combined. Divide batter among prepared pans.

Bake until a wooden pick inserted in center comes out clean, 35 to 45 minutes. Let cool in pans for 10 minutes. Run a knife around edges of pans to loosen cakes. Remove from pans, and let cool completely on wire racks. Serve with jam, if desired.

*We used Swans Down.

Cinnamon Roll Pound Cake

Cake

- ¾ cup unsalted butter, softened
- ½ cup butter-flavored shortening
- 2 cups granulated sugar
- 4 large eggs, room temperature
- 2¼ cups sifted cake flour
- 2 teaspoons baking powder
- 2 teaspoons ground cinnamon, divided
- 1 teaspoon salt
- ¾ cup sour cream
- ⅓ cup half-and-half
- 3 teaspoons vanilla extract, divided
- ⅓ cup firmly packed light brown sugar
- ⅓ cup unsalted butter, melted
- 2 teaspoons all-purpose flour
- Cream Cheese Glaze (recipe follows)

Cream Cheese Glaze
Makes about 1½ cups

- 1 (8-ounce) package cream cheese, softened
- ½ cup confectioners' sugar
- ¼ cup heavy whipping cream
- ½ teaspoon vanilla extract

Preheat oven to 325°. Spray a 10x5-inch loaf pan with baking spray with flour; line bottom of pan with parchment paper.

Cake: In a large bowl, beat butter, shortening, and granulated sugar with a mixer at medium speed until fluffy, 3 to 4 minutes, stopping to scrape sides of bowl. Add eggs, one at a time, beating well after each addition.

In a medium bowl, whisk together flour, baking powder, 1 teaspoon cinnamon, and salt. In a small bowl, whisk together sour cream, half-and-half, and 2 teaspoons vanilla. Reduce mixer speed to low. Gradually add flour mixture to butter mixture alternately with sour cream mixture, beginning and ending with flour mixture, beating just until combined after each addition.

In a small bowl, whisk together brown sugar, melted butter, flour, remaining 1 teaspoon cinnamon, and remaining 1 teaspoon vanilla.

Pour one-fourth of batter into prepared pan. Sprinkle one-fourth of cinnamon sugar mixture over batter. Pull a knife through batter to create a swirl pattern. Repeat procedure three times, alternating batter and cinnamon sugar mixture, swirling after each addition.

Bake until a wooden pick inserted in center comes out clean, about 1 hour and 15 minutes, covering with foil halfway through baking to prevent excess browning. Let cool in pan for 10 minutes. Remove from pan, and let cool completely on a wire rack. Drizzle Cream Cheese Glaze over cooled cake. Store covered at room temperature for up to 3 days.

Cream Cheese Glaze: In a medium bowl, beat cream cheese and confectioners' sugar with a mixer at medium speed until smooth, about 3 minutes. With mixer on medium-high speed, add cream and vanilla, beating until smooth. Use immediately.

Coconut Pound Cake

MAKES 1 (9X5-INCH) LOAF

Cake
¾ cup unsalted butter, softened
½ (8-ounce) package cream cheese, softened
1½ cups granulated sugar
3 large eggs
2 teaspoons vanilla extract
1 teaspoon coconut extract
1½ cups all-purpose flour
1 teaspoon salt
½ teaspoon baking powder
½ teaspoon lemon zest
Coconut Glaze (recipe follows)
Garnish: fresh coconut shavings

Coconut Glaze
Makes 1 cup
2 cups confectioners' sugar
¼ cup unsweetened coconut milk
1 tablespoon fresh lemon juice

Preheat oven to 350°. Spray a 9x5-inch loaf pan with baking spray with flour.

Cake: In the bowl of a stand mixer fitted with the paddle attachment, beat butter and cream cheese at medium speed until smooth. Add sugar, and beat until fluffy, 3 to 4 minutes, stopping to scrape sides of bowl. Add eggs, one at a time, beating well after each addition. Beat in extracts.

In a medium bowl, stir together flour, salt, baking powder, and zest. Reduce mixer speed to low. Gradually add flour mixture to butter mixture, beating just until combined. Spoon batter into prepared pan.

Bake until a wooden pick inserted in center comes out clean, about 1 hour and 5 minutes. Let cool in pan for 10 minutes. Remove from pan, and let cool completely on a wire rack. Pour Coconut Glaze over cooled cake. Garnish with coconut shavings, if desired.

Coconut Glaze: In a small bowl, whisk together confectioners' sugar, coconut milk, and lemon juice until smooth. Use immediately.

Glazed Lemon, Poppy Seed and Thyme Cake

MAKES 2 (8X4-INCH) LOAVES

Cake

2	cups unsalted butter, softened
2	cups granulated sugar
2	tablespoons poppy seeds
2	tablespoons chopped fresh thyme
4	large eggs, room temperature
1½	cups all-purpose flour
1½	cups cake flour
1	teaspoon baking powder
¼	teaspoon salt
1	cup whole buttermilk, room temperature
1	teaspoon lemon zest
2	tablespoons fresh lemon juice
1	teaspoon vanilla extract

Lemon Glaze (recipe follows)
Garnish: fresh thyme, lemon slices

Lemon Glaze
Makes about 1¼ cups

1	cup confectioners' sugar
¼	cup fresh lemon juice

Preheat oven to 350°. Spray 2 (8x4-inch) loaf pans with baking spray with flour.

Cake: In a large bowl, beat butter and sugar with a mixer at medium speed until creamy, 3 to 4 minutes, stopping to scrape sides of bowl. Add poppy seeds and thyme, beating until combined. Add eggs, one at a time, beating well after each addition.

In another large bowl, sift together flours, baking powder, and salt. In a small bowl, whisk together buttermilk, lemon zest and juice, and vanilla. Reduce mixer speed to low. Gradually add flour mixture to butter mixture alternately with buttermilk mixture, beginning and ending with flour mixture, beating just until combined after each addition. Divide batter between prepared pans.

Bake for 30 minutes. Cover with foil, and bake until a wooden pick inserted in center comes out clean, 30 to 45 minutes more. Let cool in pans for 10 minutes. Remove from pans, and let cool completely on a wire rack. Pour Lemon Glaze over cooled loaves. Garnish with thyme and lemon slices, if desired.

Lemon Glaze: In a small bowl, whisk together confectioners' sugar and lemon juice until smooth. Use immediately.

Strawberry Cream Cheese Pound Cake

MAKES 2 (8X4-INCH) LOAVES

Cake
1   (8-ounce) package cream
      cheese, softened
1   cup unsalted butter,
      softened
3   cups sugar
6   large eggs
1   tablespoon vanilla extract
3½ cups all-purpose flour
¼   teaspoon baking powder
½   teaspoon salt
1   cup heavy whipping cream
Strawberry Sauce
      (recipe follows)
Fresh strawberries and
      sweetened whipped
      cream, to serve

Strawberry Sauce
Makes about 1 cup
1   pint fresh strawberries
2   tablespoons water
1   tablespoon cornstarch
3   tablespoons sugar

Preheat oven to 325°. Spray 2 (8x4-inch) loaf pans with baking spray with flour.

Cake: In a large bowl, beat cream cheese and butter with a mixer at medium speed until creamy. Add sugar; beat until fluffy, 3 to 4 minutes, stopping to scrape sides of bowl. Add eggs, one at a time, beating well after each addition. Beat in vanilla.

In another large bowl, sift together flour, baking powder, and salt. Reduce mixer speed to low. Gradually add flour mixture to butter mixture alternately with cream, beginning and ending with flour mixture, beating just until combined after each addition. Transfer half of batter to a medium bowl; set aside.

Spoon one-third of remaining batter into one prepared pan. Place ¼ cup Strawberry Sauce in center of batter. Repeat layers once; top with remaining one-third of batter. Using a wooden skewer, gently swirl batter. Repeat process in remaining pan with remaining batter and remaining Strawberry Sauce. Tap pans on counter twice to release air bubbles.

Bake until a wooden pick inserted in center comes out clean, about 1 hour and 10 minutes. Let cool in pans for 10 minutes. Remove from pans, and let cool completely on a wire rack. Serve with strawberries and whipped cream, if desired.

Strawberry Sauce: In the work bowl of a food processor, pulse strawberries until smooth, about 1 minute.

In a small bowl, whisk together 2 tablespoons water and cornstarch until smooth.

In a medium saucepan, heat puréed strawberries and sugar over medium-high heat. Whisk in cornstarch mixture. Bring to a boil; cook, stirring constantly, until thickened, about 1 minute.

Lemon-Cornmeal Pound Cake

MAKES 2 (9X5-INCH) LOAVES

Cake
3	cups all-purpose flour
½	cup plain yellow cornmeal
1	teaspoon baking powder
½	teaspoon salt
2	cups unsalted butter, softened
2	cups granulated sugar
6	large eggs
1	cup whole milk
1	teaspoon vanilla extract
3	teaspoons lemon zest, divided

Glaze
2	cups confectioners' sugar
2	tablespoons fresh lemon juice
4 to 6	tablespoons whole milk

Fresh peach slices and sweetened whipped cream, to serve

Preheat oven to 325°. Spray 2 (9x5-inch) loaf pans with baking spray with flour.

Cake: In a medium bowl, combine flour, cornmeal, baking powder, and salt; stir well. In a large bowl, beat butter and sugar with a mixer at medium speed until fluffy, 3 to 4 minutes, stopping to scrape sides of bowl. Add eggs, one at a time, beating well after each addition.

Reduce mixer speed to low. Gradually add flour mixture to butter mixture alternately with milk, beginning and ending with flour mixture, beating just until combined after each addition. Add vanilla and 1 teaspoon zest, beating just until combined. (Batter will be thick.) Divide batter between prepared pans.

Bake until a wooden pick inserted in center comes out clean, 60 to 65 minutes. Let cool in pans for 10 minutes. Remove from pans, and let cool completely on a wire rack.

Glaze: In a small bowl, whisk together confectioners' sugar, lemon juice, and 2 tablespoons milk until smooth, adding remaining milk to achieve a thin consistency, if necessary. Drizzle Glaze over cakes, and sprinkle with remaining 2 teaspoons zest. Serve with peaches and whipped cream, if desired.

Sweet Potato-Cream Cheese Pound Cake

MAKES 2 (9X5-INCH) LOAVES

1 (8-ounce) package cream cheese, softened
½ cup unsalted butter, softened
1 cup firmly packed light brown sugar
1 cup granulated sugar
4 large eggs
1½ cups peeled grated sweet potato
3 cups self-rising flour
1½ teaspoons pumpkin pie spice
1 teaspoon vanilla extract

Preheat oven to 350°. Spray 2 (9x5-inch) loaf pans with baking spray with flour.

In a large bowl, beat cream cheese and butter with a mixer at medium speed until creamy. Add sugars; beat until fluffy, 3 to 4 minutes, stopping to scrape sides of bowl. Add eggs, one at a time, beating well after each addition. Add sweet potato, beating until combined.

In a medium bowl, whisk together flour and pumpkin pie spice. Reduce mixer speed to low. Gradually add flour mixture to sweet potato mixture, beating just until combined. Beat in vanilla. Divide batter between prepared pans.

Bake until a wooden pick inserted in center comes out clean, about 45 minutes. Let cool in pans 10 minutes. Remove from pans, and let cool completely on a wire rack.

Vanilla Bean Pound Cake

¾ cup unsalted butter, softened
1½ cups sugar
4 large eggs
1½ cups all-purpose flour
¼ teaspoon salt
½ cup heavy whipping cream
1 vanilla bean, split lengthwise, seeds scraped and reserved
1½ teaspoons vanilla extract
Sweetened whipped cream and fresh berries, to serve

Preheat oven to 300°. Spray 2 (9x5-inch) loaf pans with baking spray with flour.

In a large bowl, beat butter and sugar with a mixer at medium speed until fluffy, 3 to 4 minutes, stopping to scrape sides of bowl. Add eggs, one at a time, beating well after each addition.

In a medium bowl, sift together flour and salt. Reduce mixer speed to low. Gradually add flour mixture to butter mixture alternately with cream, beginning and ending with flour mixture, beating just until combined after each addition. Add vanilla bean seeds and vanilla extract, beating to combine. Divide batter between prepared pans.

Bake for 1 hour. Cover loosely with foil, and bake until a wooden pick inserted in center comes out clean, 5 to 10 minutes more. Let cool in pans for 15 minutes. Remove from pans, and let cool completely on a wire rack. Serve with whipped cream and fresh berries, if desired.

Strawberry Shortcake Pound Cake

1 cup unsalted butter, softened
2 cups sugar
5 large eggs
1 tablespoon strawberry extract
½ teaspoon vanilla extract
2¼ cups all-purpose flour
½ teaspoon salt
1 cup chopped fresh strawberries
½ cup sour cream
Sliced fresh strawberries, strawberry syrup, and sweetened whipped cream, to serve
Garnish: toasted chopped almonds, fresh mint sprigs

Preheat oven to 350°. Spray a 10x5-inch loaf pan with baking spray with flour.

In a large bowl, beat butter and sugar with a mixer at medium speed until fluffy, 3 to 4 minutes, stopping to scrape sides of bowl. Add eggs, one at a time, beating well after each addition. Beat in extracts.

In a medium bowl, whisk together flour and salt. Reduce mixer speed to low. Gradually add flour mixture to butter mixture, beating just until combined. Stir in chopped strawberries and sour cream. Spoon batter into prepared pan.

Bake for 1 hour. Cover loosely with foil, and bake until a wooden pick inserted in center comes out clean, 40 to 45 minutes more. Let cool in pan for 10 minutes. Remove from pan, and let cool completely on a wire rack. Serve with sliced strawberries, strawberry syrup, and whipped cream. Garnish with almonds and mint, if desired.

Pound Cake with Berries and Nectarines

3 large eggs
¼ cup whole milk
2 teaspoons vanilla extract
1½ cups cake flour
¾ cup sugar
1 teaspoon baking powder
¼ teaspoon salt
¾ cup unsalted butter, softened
4 cups sliced fresh nectarines
1 cup fresh blackberries
1 cup fresh blueberries
¼ cup honey
2 tablespoons almond-flavored liqueur
1 teaspoon orange zest
Sweetened whipped cream, to serve

Preheat oven to 350°. Spray a 9x5-inch loaf pan with baking spray with flour.

In a medium bowl, whisk together eggs, milk, and vanilla. In a large bowl, stir together flour, sugar, baking powder, and salt. Add butter and half of egg mixture to flour mixture; beat with a mixer at low speed until combined. Increase mixer speed to medium-high; beat until fluffy, about 1 minute. Scrape sides of bowl, and add remaining egg mixture, ¼ cup at a time, beating well after each addition. Spoon batter into prepared pan, smoothing top with an offset spatula.

Bake until a wooden pick inserted in center comes out clean, about 1 hour. Let cool in pan for 10 minutes. Remove from pan, and let cool completely on a wire rack.

In a medium bowl, stir together nectarines, berries, honey, liqueur, and zest. Let stand for 5 minutes. Serve over pound cake with whipped cream, if desired.

Honey-Orange Loaf Pound Cakes

MAKES 4 (5X3X2-INCH) LOAVES

Cake

1¾ cups cake flour
1 cup granulated sugar
2 teaspoons baking powder
¼ teaspoon salt
½ cup vegetable oil
½ cup fresh orange juice
2 tablespoons honey
4 large egg whites
2 tablespoons confectioners' sugar
Orange Glaze (recipe follows)

Orange Glaze
Makes about 2 cups
2 cups confectioners' sugar
¼ cup fresh orange juice
2 tablespoons honey

Preheat oven to 350°. Spray 4 (5x3x2-inch) loaf pans with baking spray with flour.

Cake: In a large bowl, sift together flour, sugar, baking powder, and salt. Add oil, orange juice, and honey, whisking until smooth.

In a small bowl, beat egg whites with a mixer at high speed until soft peaks form. Gradually add confectioners' sugar, beating until stiff peaks form. Gently fold into batter. Divide batter among prepared pans.

Bake until a wooden pick inserted in center comes out clean, 20 to 25 minutes. Let cool in pans for 10 minutes. Remove from pans, and let cool completely on a wire rack. Pour Orange Glaze over cakes.

Orange Glaze: In a large bowl, whisk together confectioners' sugar, orange juice, and honey until smooth.

Baby Carrot Pound Cakes

MAKES 4 INDIVIDUAL TIERED CAKES

Cake
1½   cups unsalted butter, softened
1½   cups superfine sugar
6   large eggs, room temperature
1½   teaspoons vanilla extract
1   teaspoon lemon zest
2¾   cups plus 2 tablespoons sifted cake flour
1   tablespoon baking powder
½   teaspoon ground ginger
¼   teaspoon salt
1⅓   cups shredded baby carrots, squeezed dry
Pourable Cream Cheese Frosting (recipe follows)
Garnish: carrot rosettes, fresh mint

Pourable Cream Cheese Frosting
Makes 6 to 7 cups
2   (8-ounce) packages cream cheese, softened
1¼   cups warm water
¾   cup powdered milk
1½   teaspoons clear vanilla extract
5   cups confectioners' sugar
Apricot food coloring paste

Preheat oven to 325°. Spray a 4-well multi-tier cake pan with baking spray with flour.

Cake: In a large bowl, beat butter and sugar with a mixer at medium speed until creamy, 3 to 4 minutes, stopping to scrape sides of bowl. Add eggs, one at a time, beating well after each addition. Beat in vanilla and zest.

In a medium bowl, sift together flour, baking powder, ginger, and salt. Reduce mixer speed to low. Gradually add flour mixture to butter mixture, beating just until combined. Gently fold in carrots. Divide batter among prepared wells. Tap pan on counter to release any air bubbles.

Bake until golden brown and a wooden pick inserted in center comes out clean, about 45 minutes. Let cool in pan for 5 minutes. Remove from pan, and let cool completely on a wire rack. Pour Pourable Cream Cheese Frosting over each cake to coat. Let dry, and coat again. Garnish with carrot rosettes and mint, if desired.

Pourable Cream Cheese Frosting: In a large bowl, beat cream cheese with a mixer at medium-high speed until smooth. Add 1¼ cups warm water, powdered milk, and vanilla, beating until combined. Gradually add confectioners' sugar, 1 cup at a time, beating until desired consistency is reached. Add a small amount of food coloring paste until desired color is reached.

cake tip

Apricot food coloring paste
is available at cake-decorating
supply stores.

Jo's Whipping Cream Pound Cakes

MAKES 12

1 cup unsalted butter
3 cups granulated sugar
5 large eggs
3 cups cake flour
1 cup heavy whipping cream
1½ teaspoons pure vanilla extract
Garnish: confectioners' sugar, sliced fresh strawberries

Preheat oven to 325°. Spray 12 (1½-cup) ramekins with baking spray with flour.

In a large bowl, beat butter and granulated sugar with a mixer at medium speed until fluffy, 3 to 4 minutes, stopping to scrape sides of bowl. Add eggs, one at a time, beating well after each addition.

Reduce mixer speed to low. Gradually add flour to butter mixture alternately with cream, beginning and ending with flour, beating just until combined after each addition. Beat in vanilla. Divide batter among prepared ramekins.

Bake until a wooden pick inserted in center comes out clean, 30 to 35 minutes. Let cool completely on a wire rack. Garnish with confectioners' sugar and strawberries, if desired.

Orange-Cream Cheese Pound Cakes

MAKES 12

1   (8-ounce) package cream
     cheese, softened
1   cup unsalted butter,
     softened
1½   cups sugar
4   large eggs
2   tablespoons orange zest
3   tablespoons fresh orange
     juice
2¼   cups all-purpose flour
1   teaspoon baking powder
½   teaspoon salt
½   teaspoon ground
     cardamom
2   oranges, peeled and thinly
     sliced
Sugar, for caramelizing

Preheat oven to 325°. Spray 12 (1½-cup) ramekins with baking spray with flour.

In the bowl of a stand mixer fitted with the paddle attachment, beat cream cheese and butter at medium speed until creamy. Add sugar; beat until fluffy, 3 to 4 minutes, stopping to scrape sides of bowl. Add eggs, one at a time, beating well after each addition. Beat in orange zest and juice.

In a medium bowl, whisk together flour, baking powder, salt, and cardamom. Reduce mixer speed to low. Gradually add flour mixture to butter mixture, beating just until combined. Spoon batter into prepared ramekins, filling each three-fourths full.

Bake until a wooden pick inserted in center comes out clean, 30 to 35 minutes. Let cool completely in pans.

Just before serving, arrange orange slices over cooled cakes. Sprinkle each with about 1 tablespoon sugar. Using a kitchen torch, caramelize oranges. Serve immediately.

Bittersweet Mini Bundt Cakes with Brandied Whipped Cream

MAKES 6

Cake
- ¼ cup unsweetened cocoa powder
- ¼ cup boiling water
- 2 teaspoons espresso powder or instant coffee
- 1 cup unsalted butter
- ⅔ cup granulated sugar
- ⅔ cup firmly packed light brown sugar
- 1½ teaspoons vanilla extract
- 3 large eggs
- 1⅔ cups all-purpose flour
- 1 teaspoon baking powder
- ½ teaspoon salt
- 2 ounces bittersweet chocolate, melted and cooled

Bittersweet Chocolate Glaze (recipe follows)
Brandied Whipped Cream (recipe follows)
Garnish: ground cinnamon

Bittersweet Chocolate Glaze
Makes about 1 cup
- 1 (4-ounce) bar bittersweet chocolate, finely chopped
- ½ cup heavy whipping cream
- ½ teaspoon vanilla extract

Brandied Whipped Cream
Makes about 3 cups
- 1 cup heavy whipping cream
- 2 tablespoons confectioners' sugar
- 2 tablespoons brandy
- ½ teaspoon vanilla extract

Preheat oven to 325°. Spray a 6-mold miniature fluted tube pan* with baking spray with flour.

Cake: In a small bowl, whisk together cocoa, ¼ cup boiling water, and espresso powder until smooth. Let stand until cooled to room temperature.

In a large bowl, beat butter, sugars, and vanilla with a mixer at medium speed until fluffy, 3 to 4 minutes, stopping to scrape sides of bowl. Add eggs, one at a time, beating well after each addition.

In a medium bowl, whisk together flour, baking powder, and salt. Reduce mixer speed to low. Gradually add flour mixture and cocoa mixture to butter mixture, beating until combined. Beat in melted chocolate. (Batter will be thick.) Spoon batter into prepared molds, smoothing tops using an offset spatula. Tap pan on counter twice to release air bubbles.

Bake until a wooden pick inserted near center comes out clean, about 25 minutes. Let cool in pan for 10 minutes. Remove from pan, and let cool on a wire rack for 30 minutes. Spoon Bittersweet Chocolate Glaze over cakes. Serve with Brandied Whipped Cream. Garnish with cinnamon, if desired.

Bittersweet Chocolate Glaze: Place chopped chocolate in a medium bowl. In a small saucepan, heat cream to a simmer over medium heat. Pour over chocolate, stirring until smooth. Stir in vanilla. Use immediately.

Brandied Whipped Cream: In a medium bowl, beat cream, confectioners' sugar, brandy, and vanilla with a mixer at high speed until soft peaks form. Use immediately, or cover and refrigerate for up to 1 hour.

*We used Wilton Excelle Elite Mini Fluted Tube Pan.

Orange Cardamom Loaves

MAKES 2 (8X4-INCH) LOAVES

Cake
2½ cups granulated sugar
1½ cups whole milk
1   cup vegetable oil
3   large eggs
2   tablespoons orange zest
1½ teaspoons vanilla extract
3   cups all-purpose flour
1½ teaspoons salt
1½ teaspoons baking powder
¼   teaspoon ground
    cardamom
Orange Glaze (recipe follows)

Orange Glaze
Makes about 1⅓ cups
2   cups confectioners' sugar
1   teaspoon orange zest
⅓   cup fresh orange juice

Preheat oven to 350°. Spray 2 (8x4-inch) loaf pans with baking spray with flour.

Cake: In a large bowl, beat sugar, milk, oil, eggs, zest, and vanilla with a mixer at medium speed until well combined.

In a medium bowl, sift together flour, salt, baking powder, and cardamom. Reduce mixer speed to low. Gradually add flour mixture to sugar mixture, beating until smooth. Spread batter into prepared pans.

Bake for 30 minutes. Loosely cover with foil, and bake until a wooden pick inserted in center comes out clean, about 30 minutes more. Let cool in pans for 10 minutes. Remove from pans, and let cool completely on a wire rack.

Drizzle with Orange Glaze; let stand until set, about 20 minutes. Store in an airtight container for up to 3 days.

Orange Glaze: In a medium bowl, whisk together all ingredients until smooth.

index